setting up
home

the essential guide to
creating a home from scratch

To Sue

THIS IS A CARLTON BOOK

Design copyright © 2000 Carlton Books Limited
Text copyright © 2000 Lorrie Mack
This edition was published by Carlton Books Limited in 2000
20 Mortimer Street
London W1N 7RD

A CIP catalogue for this book is available from the British Library
ISBN 1 84222 016 0

Editorial Manager: **Venetia Penfold**
Art Director: **Penny Stock**
Senior Art Editor: **Barbara Zuñiga**
Designer: **Joanne Long**
Project Editor: **Zia Mattocks**
Copy Editor: **Jane Donovan**
Picture Researcher: **Alex Pepper**
Production Controller: **Janette Davis**

Printed and bound in Dubai

setting up
home

the essential guide to
creating a home from scratch

Lorrie Mack

CARLTON
BOOKS

CONTENTS

introduction **6**

making your home your own

rooms to live in

INTRODUCTION

Like many major life events, acquiring your first home inspires an intoxicating mix of excitement at the possibilities it offers, and anxiety at the responsibility it all entails. Whether you begin your independent life in a rented flat or a property you've bought, by yourself or with a partner, one of its most thrilling aspects is the freedom to create a domestic environment tailored exclusively to your tastes, your needs and your way of life.

Like any other subject area, however, the world of design and furnishing has its own vocabulary, priorities, assumptions and values that can easily overwhelm the inexperienced. From knowing instinctively that you want your home to be stylish, comfortable and efficient, it can seem a very big leap indeed to creating sympathetic and practical design schemes, choosing all your major furnishings and fittings, and understanding the difference between one type of pillow or saucepan and another. The whole operation involves not only large sums of money, but also considerable time and energy, both physical and emotional, so even small mistakes can lead to waste, delay, inconvenience and disappointment.

Set against immaculate surfaces and subtly stylish hues, a few well-designed furnishing items are all that's needed to create a dramatic and comfortable living space. Here, the classic lamp spotlighting the spiral storage unit is easily swivelled towards the chair or sofa to illuminate a cosy reading corner.

information & guidance

This book is very much a beginner's guide to setting up home; a first reference source intended to demystify the whole subject and help you to take the right decisions and identify the choices that work best for you. It will show you how to make the best and most flexible use of your space; how to develop your own individual look and create it successfully; how to prioritize purchases, tasks and resources; and how to get the very best value for your money at a time when a huge number of demands are being made on it. For each room in turn, it sketches out the range of functions you will need to cater for, anticipates the problems you're likely to encounter and suggests workable solutions, and provides a wealth of achievable design options, ideas and tips to inspire you. Where appropriate, it also includes basic equipment lists and buying guides to a wide variety of essential items such as beds, carpets and tableware, along with notes about care, safety and environmental issues.

In order to build up a usable frame of reference and a clear picture of what's ahead, try to read through all the chapters first before you get too immersed in the work at hand. If that's not possible, at least leaf through the book and familiarize yourself with its structure, so that when a problem crops up or a decision has to be made, you'll know where to look.

finding your way

In some cases, the information you unearth — and the enthusiasm with which you respond to it — will set you off in search of further, more detailed and specialist reference material. If your imagination has been captured by a particular design style (for example, an exotic eastern fantasy or a playful retro homage), or you find yourself fascinated by a specific element of decoration (paint and paint effects, maybe, or elaborate window treatments), there is a vast range of books, magazines, videos, CD ROMs, DVDs and websites available for you to explore in depth.

Some people get enormous satisfaction from taking on practical tasks themselves, from stripping floors and building cupboards to sewing curtains or hanging wallpaper. For many others, self-help is a sheer economic necessity. If you have already mastered a basic repertoire of skills, the ideas and images that follow should inspire you to put them to extensive and rewarding use. Even those who have never dabbled in DIY before, though, will be able to manage many of the techniques mentioned. To provide an idea of how complicated or difficult you're likely to find some of them, the relevant section includes a rough outline of what's involved. Please note, though, that these informal descriptions are not intended to take the place of either expert tuition or the comprehensive information and step-by-step instructions contained in a good reference manual. And accept that there are some jobs (anything to do with structural alterations, heating, electricity and plumbing, for example) that are too large, too technical and much too dangerous to be undertaken by anyone other than a professional or an extremely skilled and experienced amateur.

common sense & confidence

Before you make any purchase, from a tin of paint or a set of cutlery to a washing machine or a sofa, take time to survey the market and firm up your ideas about what you want. If there are any gaps in your knowledge or your understanding, don't be afraid to ask questions in the shops or showrooms where you've been browsing. When you do buy something you're not completely familiar with, read everything that's printed on the packaging or in any accompanying leaflets. In every product area, manufacturers invest vast sums of money in establishing the optimum conditions of use and/or care for their goods, so it makes sense to take advantage of their expertise. Above all, never try to cut corners by ignoring or skimping on safety precautions: you may be putting your home – or even your life – at risk.

Inevitably, the adventure you face will have its own highs and lows: times when progress is slow and inspiration is elusive, and moments when your ideas come to life and your spirits soar. In the end, what you stand to gain is a private sanctuary that fulfils your practical needs, reflects your personality, recharges your batteries and soothes your spirit: a real home.

Distinctive accessories and personal details often give a room its personality. A surprisingly traditional bedside table and a sophisticated collection of touchy-feely textiles transform this basically neutral bedroom corner into a sleek and inviting chill zone.

1

When you take on your first home, you're bound to get excited by things like colour schemes and furnishings. Before you reach this stage, though, it's important to evaluate your property in its original, empty state to see if you

the basic shell

can improve its looks, its function, or the degree to which it reflects your personality. Some jobs should be tackled for practical reasons, some are justified in terms of comfort or convenience, and others are purely a matter of aesthetics. Decisions about which ones to take on will be governed by the condition of your rooms, the depth of your purse and whether you're renting or buying.

SETTING
YOUR SCENE

Before you plan any major alterations or design schemes, take a good look at the space you have available and think about how you can make the best use of it. One of the simplest ways to do this is to reassign the function of some of the rooms. If the main bedroom, for instance, receives more light and has a prettier view than the living room, consider swapping them around. This solution often works in multistorey houses, where the living room is traditionally situated on the ground floor with the bedrooms above. In the same way, an older house with a basement kitchen might be improved enormously if the food preparation area were on the ground floor instead, near the main areas of activity and entertaining, while the bedroom, where isolation and absence of light are less problematic, is transferred to the basement.

Shifting the living area from its conventional position beside the front door to the back of the house may mean that the room can be opened out onto the garden all day and you are also protected from the prying eyes of passers-by. You could even replace one of the larger windows with doors to create direct access. Try moving the kitchen or bedroom to the front of the house in its place. Another option is to combine functions in different ways; for example, if you work from home and there isn't room for an office, the obvious solution is to set one up in the living room or the bedroom. It may be more sensible, however, to make one room into a studio where you sleep and relax, and the other into a full-time work environment. This arrangement encourages total concentration during the day (and gives a professional impression to visiting clients), and makes it much easier to detach completely after working hours. Similarly, installing a stylish kitchen at one end of a spacious living room creates a convenient multifunctional interior and frees the original kitchen area for use as either an office or guest room or both. The trick here is to think about what you want from your home instead of automatically accepting the status quo. In the end, if the original plan seems to be the best, stick with it; there's nothing to be gained from change for its own sake.

sound structure

If you own your home, and especially if you've bought an older property, you may face the expense and inconvenience of basic building work at the very beginning. Some of the jobs that come into this category, those involving the structure of the property itself or essential services, such as electricity and plumbing, are a matter of necessity rather than choice. Although some work can conceivably be put off for two or three years, if possible it's worth making every effort to get it out of the way at the start. Otherwise, if you're still there when

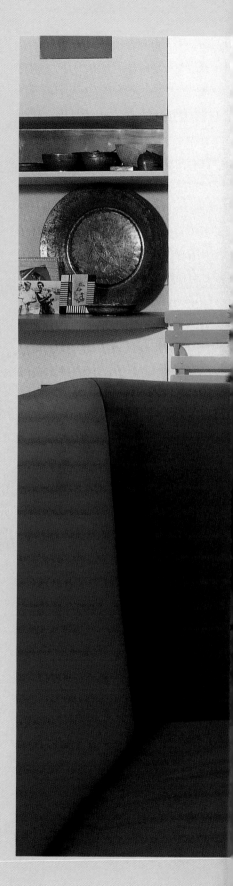

Rethinking the purpose and the structure of your rooms can often enhance the efficiency as well as the appearance of your home, and allow you to accommodate more activities than you ever thought possible.

USING AN ARCHITECT

Deciding how much and what kind of changes to make to your new home can be very daunting indeed. To take away some of the stress, consider enlisting the help of a professional architect or designer. The best way to find one is through personal recommendation; if that's not possible, contact the appropriate professional association, who will provide a list of suitable local firms. In some cases, you may be able to commission just a set of drawings (essentially, you pay for the ideas), then it's up to you to organize the job yourself. Usually, though, in addition to designing the space, your professional will hire the builders, order in materials and generally oversee the project. Good architects give excellent value for money as they can spot the hidden potential in any building and often find ingenious solutions to seemingly insurmountable problems. They will advise you of any planning regulations that relate to the work you want to carry out and may save you money by recommending low-cost methods and materials, buying items at trade price and applying for appropriate grants and subsidies. Finally, and perhaps most importantly of all, they can help you to avoid making cripplingly expensive mistakes.

the time comes to carry the work out, the mess and disruption to your lovingly decorated rooms may be enormous. And if you decide to sell your home in the meantime, the overall value of your property will almost certainly be strongly affected by clapped-out wiring or a dodgy roof.

Bear in mind that every major task you undertake provides additional scope for creating your ideal environment. If, for example, you are faced with installing a new heating system, explore all the available options first before making any decisions. Perhaps you can accommodate an unobtrusive, energy-efficient underfloor system, one that blows warm air through ducts into each room or one that releases heat through narrow perimeter grilles set into the floor or the skirting boards. The major advantage of all these systems over radiators is that they are visually unobtrusive and impose minimum restrictions on the placement of furniture. Should you inherit a perfectly efficient heating system that has boring, ugly radiators already in place, replace them with more alluring alternatives. Choose from modern graphic designs, wrap a radiator around a column or explore the possibility of repositioning your existing radiators to make much better use of the space.

When rewiring is necessary, take the opportunity to install additional power points in every room; enough to cater for floor and table lights, a television, video and sound system, plus a computer, fax, answering machine and appliances less frequently used, such as a hairdryer and vacuum cleaner. In the kitchen especially, a generous allocation of electrical outlets is essential, since trailing flexes are dangerous as well as inconvenient and unsightly.

major alterations

In addition to essential tasks, there is a wide range of elective changes that can make a huge difference to both the look of your home and its comfort and efficiency. At one end of the scale in terms of cost, time and complexity are options such as adding an extension or converting a previously uninhabitable basement or attic. Few first-time buyers are in a position to consider large-scale projects such as these, but if you have the resources available, getting the work done before you move in may prove to be a wise step.

Slightly less overwhelming ideas that will still improve your property dramatically include adding extra floor space in the form of a mezzanine or gallery fitted over a lofty stairwell or room, or installing an extra cloakroom. If you plan to accommodate lots of visiting friends (overnight, for weekends or longer stays) or take in short-term lodgers to help with the mortgage, an ensuite bathroom would be an invaluable facility. One of the most popular structural alterations is to knock two rooms into a single, much larger one. Common examples of this are combined living and dining rooms, living rooms and entrance halls, kitchens and dining rooms, and even bedrooms and bathrooms. On the plus side, this tactic creates an enormously enhanced feeling of space and light, and it offers maximum flexibility of use. The extensive floor area lends itself to more varied and imposing styles of furniture and gives greater scope for placement. Opening space in this way often makes far more sensible use of dwellings intended for a way of life that has long disappeared, when heat from open fires had to be enclosed, servants beavered away in remote kitchens and gentlemen retired to the drawing room after dinner.

For those who live alone, the only real drawback is a lack of environmental variety. When two or more people live together, however, it's important to think about the daily reality open-plan living entails, as well its undoubted aesthetic appeal. Creating a single space out of several smaller ones severely limits the potential for solitude and privacy, and makes it harder to carry out different activities simultaneously. And any untidiness is not only immediately obvious but also more difficult to hide away.

Another structural alteration that can affect both style and space is replacing an existing staircase. By installing one with the same basic shape but a more contemporary design (open treads, perhaps, or a simpler handrail and balustrade), the setting may be transformed. Choosing a different type altogether – a spiral staircase, for example, instead of a conventional dog-leg shape – may also release valuable floor space. Before you decide to do this, however, make sure your plans allow sufficient access for large items of furniture, or explore the possibility of hoisting them up through the windows of the upper floor.

Left: When you want a change from uninspiring standard radiators, choose a sculptural contemporary design (left), or a traditional chunky model in cast iron, either new or reconditioned.

USING BUILDERS

Finding good builders is the most important element of any project. Again, try to get personal recommendations. Put in writing exactly what you want done and ask several firms for a quotation. (Bear in mind that while a quotation is firm and binding, an estimate is only that – the final price can change.) Try to inspect previous jobs and talk to clients; responsible tradesmen will always arrange this for you. Reliable builders, too, should provide you with an office (or even home) address and phone number; those who can be reached only by mobile may not be trustworthy.

Avoid making a decision on the basis of price alone (good builders cost more than cowboys), and expect to be asked for a deposit and staged payments to cover the cost of materials. Demands for large sums upfront, however, should set off alarm bells. Don't expect work to start immediately, since the best builders are booked up well in advance. Once the work is commissioned, budget for more money (and time) than you think you'll need; inevitably, circumstances (and ideas) change and problems crop up, and you cannot expect the resulting costs to be included in the initial price.

This page: Like a painter's canvas, your walls need to be in prime condition to provide an appropriate backdrop for your scheme. Here, a soft ochre colourwash on smooth plaster sets off the rich warmth of wood and the subtle texture of craft pottery.

Right: The sleek elegance of a lovingly restored marble fireplace provides the perfect link between period architecture and an unmistakably contemporary furnishing style.

restoration
& repair

Once you've decided on the large-scale changes you want, turn your attention to any architectural detailing, whether it is in poor condition or missing altogether. Under this heading come the skirting board, the architrave around the doors and windows, and any decorative staircase woodwork. Period features in particular are often adorned with elaborate dado and picture rails, and intricate plasterwork in the form of cornice moulding and ceiling roses. These decorative elements tend to become clogged with ancient layers of paint that blur their original design and give an overwhelming impression of shabbiness and neglect. If possible, it's worth stripping away the paint. Modern chemical strippers take away most of the hard work and mess involved in this task (work in a well-ventilated room and follow the manufacturer's instructions carefully). However, if removing the paint proves impossible, replace the damaged feature with a new version in a style appropriate to the date of the building.

One period fitting that never loses its appeal is the fireplace. If you're lucky enough to have an attractive one already in place, seek professional advice to ensure all its components are complete and in good condition. Plain or patterned tiles in the surround or on the hearth (or anywhere else, such as the bathroom or kitchen) can be cleaned and re-grouted, or replaced. If the original fireplace has long disappeared, your options are to replace it with a re-conditioned antique, a new reproduction or an unashamedly modern reworking of the theme in the form of a simple, sculptural recess – on its own or topped with a chunky timber or stone mantel shelf.

Before you can think about lighting a fire, though, seek professional advice to confirm that your chimney is sound and have it swept. Although modern fake fireplaces with gas-fuelled flames are appealingly lifelike and considerably less trouble than the originals, they still require some kind of ventilation.

If any of your floors are covered with what is obviously not original linoleum, vinyl or hardboard, investigate thoroughly what's underneath. You may discover lovely old floorboards or some other exciting surface such as parquet, stone or quarry tiles, which could be repaired and restored. Other likely candidates for repair or replacement in older properties are windows and doors. Rotting window frames not only admit draughts and cold, they also create an increased risk of damp, which can inflict serious damage to the overall fabric of a building and constitute a health hazard. Replace them with good-quality modern

frames in a suitable style and material. Ill-fitting or damaged external doors pose similar risks, but here you have the choice between buying new ones or trying to find authentic period doors of the right size. Try architectural salvage yards, which may also have suitable replacements for any internal doors that have been removed or vandalized beyond repair.

In our centrally heated homes, of course, internal doors are much less necessary than they were in times past. Doors to bathrooms and bedrooms are undoubtedly useful, but elsewhere they are often left permanently open, getting in the way and creating visual clutter. If this is likely to be the case with any of your doors, consider removing them altogether. Think about whether any of those you decide to keep could be rehung to open the other way – perhaps into a corridor instead of a bedroom. Or, if light is scarce, make the most of it by replacing solid doors with glazed ones.

If you don't have an architect or interior designer overseeing your alterations, make sure they're done in a logical order. Follow the list below:

1 Anything involving the main structure of the building, such as knocking down walls.
2 Plumbing, electrical and drainage work.
3 Plastering and repairing or replacing architectural details.
4 Carpentry jobs such as built-in shelves and cupboards.
5 Decorating with paint and/or paper. Remember that new plaster has to be left to dry out completely for several months (depending on weather conditions) before paint or wallpaper can be applied.

If in doubt, always seek professional advice on planning and structural matters before you begin any major work.

Opposite: When the look you want is clean and spare (or the existing fireplace is beyond repair), strip away the surround and replace it with a simple, solid plaster shape. This graphic take on the conventional mantel shelf provides the perfect display surface for a collection of bright, hand-blown glass.

walls & ceilings

However inconvenient it may be, try to remove old layers of wallpaper and paint before you begin to decorate. The unmistakably porridge-like surface of textured paint and paper is a particularly unsuitable basis for fresh, modern design schemes. If the plaster beneath is damaged, either arrange for a professional to repair it or cover the walls with a thick lining paper.

Inspired by the popularity of loft living, many people are attracted to the architectural look of bare brick walls. If you are tempted to strip your own walls (and this is always an unspeakably messy undertaking), remember that unlike old warehouses, many domestic buildings are constructed using unappealing grey blocks. If your heart is set on this look, however, copy the tactic used by property developers and conceal them behind brick cladding.

survival tactics

If possible, avoid living in your home while any kind of major building work is taking place. As anyone who has experienced the misery of extended periods without hot water, heat and cooking facilities, and the sinister invasion of plaster dust into every conceivable fold of flesh, fibre of fabric or toothbrush bristle will tell you, the soundness of this advice cannot be exaggerated. When occupancy is unavoidable, try to make one room at least into a civilized haven of comfort and cleanliness: somewhere you can sleep, relax, get warm (if the heating system is not functional, invest in a portable electric fire) and take refuge from the mess. If necessary, fling a coat of fresh paint over the room (even if you plan to re-decorate later) and borrow a television if you don't own one. No matter how exciting your renovation programme feels at the beginning, the overwhelming likelihood is that you will value extended and regular periods of escape before it's finished.

landlords & tenants

Those who make their first home in rented accommodation will obviously have less scope for improvement than owner-occupiers. Find out where you stand when it comes to decorations and furnishings by checking your lease or tenancy agreement. Many landlords require only that the accommodation is left in the same state as when you moved in. This may mean that you can paint the rooms as long as you return them to their original colour (or cover the cost of re-painting) when you leave. When it comes to other alterations you're not sure about – putting up shelves, for example – it's always worth asking the landlord for permission on the grounds that genuine improvements can only enhance the value of the property. It may even be possible for some costs to be shared – if, for example, you would like a particular job done, or fitting replaced when it's not strictly necessary.

Whether or not your landlord is prepared to get involved, don't rule out the idea of spending your own money. While it would be foolish to invest extravagant sums, any reasonable investment you make for your own comfort is a wise one.

2

Once you have planned your space effectively and come to grips with all the necessary repairs and restoration, you're free to get on with the most rewarding aspect of creating a home: infusing it with your own personality and flair.

finding your
style

The first stage of this process is nurturing a strong sense of your own decorating style. Then, all you need is the confidence to transform your ideas and aspirations into rooms that are not only appealing to look at, but also efficient and comfortable to live in.

CHOOSING
A LOOK

Moving into your own home involves not only social and financial independence, it also represents your first opportunity to create a completely individual domestic environment – one that reflects your tastes and enthusiasms rather than those of your parents or landlord. This new-found freedom, however exciting, can also be daunting if you don't know what you want your rooms to look like, or indeed how to find out. In fact, developing design awareness is not a complicated or mystical process. After all, few people have trouble identifying clothes they feel happy in; this is because they're used to looking at what's around and forming opinions. A sense of style in interior design comes about in the same way: by familiarizing yourself with the subject and seeking out constant and varied inspiration.

training your eye

One of the most important aspects of nurturing your visual awareness is to avoid any pressures of time. Expensive mistakes are more likely to be made (and stress levels rise dramatically) when you don't turn your mind to the relevant decisions until you're suddenly faced with choosing a kitchen or a sofa in just one weekend. Start searching for potential sources for ideas and inspiration as far ahead as possible. Magazines (and, increasingly, catalogues) are a particularly rich resource and there are a vast number of good ones on the market, so collect as many as you can afford and look through them all carefully. When you see something you like – a whole room, a piece of furniture, a fabric pattern, or even just a colour – tear out the relevant page and put it into a special file.

Explore the interior design section in two or three large bookstores or browse through the selection on the appropriate website. Again, invest as much as you can in the books you like the look of: you'll probably turn to them again and again as your ideas slowly take shape. Set aside regular chunks of your spare time to wander through the furnishing stores that appeal to you most. Exposure to the design values of even those that are beyond your budget will help to broaden your knowledge and sharpen your visual awareness. And check your local newspaper for major home-interest exhibitions, which often act as umbrella venues for a huge number of manufacturers and retailers. Wherever you go, when you are attracted to a specific range or item, pick up the relevant brochures, leaflets or photographs for your file. If a particular fabric or wallpaper sparks off your interest, ask for a small sample to take home with you.

Make a point of looking around any interesting houses that are open to the public and take away a guidebook and some postcards of those you particularly like. Start taking more notice of the rooms you see on television and in films, and try to

To someone who loves colour, clutter and cosiness, this pale room might be unappealing. For people with more ascetic tastes, however (and those whose allergies rule out abundant soft furnishings), it would be ideal.

identify the characteristics of those you particularly like or dislike. Whenever you see private homes you admire, encourage the owners to talk about them. Most people are flattered to be asked.

When you first start absorbing all these images, you may find their range and diversity overwhelming, and seemingly impossible to adapt to your own circumstances, or forge into a recognizable look. Eventually, though, a set of patterns will begin to emerge: the rooms you covet may all be light and pale, and dominated by natural textures, or cosy and warm, and filled with books and flowers, while those you perceive as cold and uninviting may have common elements such as hard floors, metal surfaces and cool hues. As your confidence grows, the separate – and sometimes disparate – responses you originally experienced will gradually turn into cohesive and well-defined tastes. A note of warning: try to avoid the desperate quest to adopt the most recent trends, acquire the latest design icons or pursue novelty for its own sake. Gimmicks very quickly become tiresome when they have no foundation in aesthetics or practicality, and almost by definition, anything that represents the extreme edge of current fashion has built-in obsolescence: it will be dated as soon as the Next Big Thing arrives. Learn to look at every trend not as a blueprint to be followed slavishly, but a source of ideas to be picked over with discrimination, and filtered through your own sensibilities. Really stylish homes are never designed in order to impress or reflect a particular set of values and aspirations. They are always firmly rooted in the personalities and interests of their occupants.

fantasy & reality

If, by the time your home is ready to be decorated, you are still unsure of what you want or unable to find it, don't be afraid to defer your decisions. Living in your space for a while can inspire your imagination, and it will certainly make you more aware not only of how you use the rooms, but also of easily overlooked factors such as how much light each one gets at different times of day. Keep in mind, too, that no design idiom, no matter how passionately you are attracted to it, is feasible if it clashes with your temperament, your circumstances, or the raw material you have to work with. Similarly, any interest that plays a large part in your life should also be taken into account; for example, a large collection of sporting memorabilia would not enhance a scheme inspired by eighteenth-century elegance.

Although there's no need to tie your style to the building's date of construction, the two elements should not be mutually exclusive; when your home is an urban loft with industrial windows, aiming for Victorian cosiness or exotic opulence is a mistake. In any case, there's no need for inappropriate choices like these. The dramatic resurgence of the home as a major focus of modern life has brought with it an unprecedented surge of creativity in the design and manufacture of domestic furnishings of every description, and more than enough inspiring and accessible ideas to accommodate any conceivable taste.

A SURVEY
OF STYLES

The vast and diverse range of potential design styles does not, of course, lend itself to tidy organization under a few headings. Picking your way through this aesthetic superabundance for the first time, however, is much less bewildering when you have some frame of reference to fall back on. This section is not a comprehensive guide to creating all these styles, but a working introduction to some of the more popular and influential examples. When you identify the ones you find most appealing, you can search out more specialist information in the form of books and magazines that focus on single, style-related subjects.

contemporary style

The dominant design movement of the twentieth century and beyond is the International Modern style. Developed by a group of architects at the Bauhaus School of Design in Germany in the early 1920s (and still the signature style of the profession), it was both a reaction to the clutter and fussiness of the previous century and a response to the advances in technology and social changes that followed the First World War. International Modern rooms are pared down and functional, but light and airy, with immaculate detail and finishing, and a studied lack of ornamentation. They are characterized by plain surfaces, neutral colours, geometric shapes and natural materials of the highest quality, such as raw silk, wood and marble. Floors are made from pale hardwood or fitted with creamy woollen carpet; smooth stone and white ceramic tiles are also typical of this look. Walls are plain plaster or brick, painted in a warm off-white and relieved only by one or two stunning pictures. Windows are hung with simple full-length curtains in a tone that blends with the floor and walls, or fitted with vertical louvre or metal Venetian blinds. Furniture is large and linear, and made from wood, glass, leather and chrome-plated tubular steel, one of the style's defining materials.

Much of the classic furniture that dominates the International Modern style is contemporary with the birth of the movement and has never been out of production. In its purest form, this look is undoubtedly an expensive one to carry off, partly due to the high cost of the appropriate furnishings and materials, but also because its characteristic emphasis on perfect detailing and flawless finishes can be achieved only with time and skill.

VARIATIONS ON A THEME

To recreate the cool tranquillity and sleek stylishness of the classic modern room on a more accessible scale, start with the elements that are neither costly nor difficult to imitate, such as pale, painted walls. For the floor, strip and wax existing boards or give them a coat of white or cream paint or colourwash (not an orange

Left: Encourage clear surfaces by removing books and other possessions to a plain and capacious storage unit. This one has strong, thick shelves with plenty of support.

Opposite: A pure white treatment brings this essentially nineteenth-century scheme up to date. The sofa's style, which originated in Austria and Germany, is called Biedermeier.

or yellowish stain or a coat of shiny varnish). Alternatively, choose short-pile carpet in a plain, light colour or a natural floor covering such as coir or sisal. Windows hung with inexpensive canvas, cotton or linen in a natural shade would suit the style perfectly. Look for upholstered seating that is large, low, simple and free of scatter cushions. Occasional chairs need not be copies of classic designs, but they should be true to their spirit: sturdy and functional with geometrical shapes. Absence of clutter is essential to this idiom so steer clear of ornaments and accessories. Neutral colours should dominate, but the odd bright splash is allowed.

If you find this very architectural look somewhat cold and inhospitable, relieve the neutral colours with sophisticated pastels, like lilac, aqua and muted grey/green, and introduce a few items of furniture with graceful curves and beautiful detailing. Define the seating area with a luxurious, long-pile rug, drape a mohair throw across the sofa and add a discreet selection of cushions with tactile covers. The secret is to avoid patterns and bright colours and to stick to more subtle shades and appealing textures.

FREE YOUR SPIRIT

If a brighter, quirkier twist on the modern theme appeals to you, start by playing with colour. Stay with a neutral palette for the major elements like the sofa and the floor; you can be more adventurous when it comes to items that can easily be changed. Look out for unusual fabrics, furnishings and accessories that reinforce the feeling you want, and try craft and flea markets to discover young designers selling their own work. The great advantage of dressing up a classic scheme is that you can revamp it as often as you like – an important factor if you want to keep up with current trends.

Another alternative is the slightly harder-edged take on contemporary style that could be described as techno chic. This look is characterized by industrial materials such as

stainless steel and zinc, chunky glass bricks, commercial shelves or lockers used for storage, studded rubber flooring and stacking chairs reminiscent of conference halls or meeting rooms. The key to cool techno chic lies in subtlety, a discreet celebration of modern materials and pure function rather than the gimmicky excesses of the 1980s hi-tech craze, when car seats became armchairs and tables were made out of oil drums.

On the whole, most styles that have their roots in the International Modern movement are more accessible, more personal and more user-friendly than the original. The most dramatic exception is minimalism, a decorating idiom so pure and uncompromising it is almost a religion. Minimalist rooms are bare of all but the most basic and sculptural furniture and of any extraneous architectural detailing such as skirting boards and cornice moulding. Lighting is recessed, electrical sockets are disguised and every item not in current use is hidden away in vast cupboards, whose handle-free doors, thanks to an ingenious touch-spring mechanism, blend invisibly into the smooth surface of the surrounding wall. Proponents of this particular ethos believe that uncluttered

space and the play of light on immaculate surfaces create an extraordinarily calm and peaceful atmosphere. Its detractors simply find it barren and cold.

period style

Through the centuries, people have lived with the furnishings and artefacts of earlier ages, either chosen for their aesthetic qualities or handed down from previous generations. The history of domestic interiors provides a rich source of decorating ideas and inspiration. Broadly, there are three ways to exploit them: aim for an authentic period scheme, re-interpret its essential qualities in your own setting, or use these qualities as a jumping-off point for a post-modern pastiche. The styles that work best are those that offer some degree of comfort and practicality as well as visual appeal. Generally, the more remote the era, the less suitable the style will be for wholesale reproduction. Remember that it's never possible (and seldom desirable) to recreate period rooms exactly, but there are enough reference books and appropriate furnishings and materials available to help you make an acceptable approximation, enhance an eclectic scheme, or provide material for a flight of historial fancy.

FORM BEFORE FUNCTION

Before the eighteenth century, homes were not regarded as somewhere to relax, so rooms tended to be cold, gloomy and sparsely furnished. Some features, though, adapt well to modern living: plain, hard floors covered with natural woven mats, walls lined with wooden panelling or hung with tapestries, simple, heavy oak furniture and creamy candles grouped together on a table or in a plain chandelier. The delicate neoclassical look, fashionable until the early part of the nineteenth century, is linked with some of the finest design and craftsmanship ever created, with its architectural references, graceful proportions, symmetrical shapes and characteristic light, clear colours, such as yellow, sky blue and more subtle greens and creams. Walls were covered with floral or striped wallpaper, or adorned with classical shapes drawn in fine moulding and colourwashed or marbled. Furniture was formal, slender and embellished with fine inlay, carving and gilding, and exquisitely framed mirrors made the most of light. Curtains were fine and filmy, while underfoot, natural floorboards were either covered with narrow strips of stitched-together carpet or dotted with oriental rugs. As the emphasis was still on appearance, sofas and chairs had only the lightest padding on seats and backs.

THE AGE OF COMFORT

Later in the nineteenth century, the elegance and restraint of neoclassicism gave way to the dramatically contrasting look that has come to be known as Victorian. As increasing importance was attached to home and family, comfort and warmth were valued as highly as aesthetics and status, so at their most successful Victorian rooms with their rich colours, luxurious textures and opulently layered patterns were infinitely welcoming. Walls and ceilings were encrusted with plasterwork and architectural detailing, with framed pictures and drawings hung in dense profusion. Textiles were elaborate, with thick velvet or brocade curtains draped and swagged at windows, and ornaments, photographs and objects were arranged on fringed cloths or runners on every surface. Furniture was typically large and heavy, with extravagant curves, and the invention of the coil spring in 1828 made possible the deeply padded and buttoned upholstery that is so much part of this look. At the heart of every room was the fireplace, its solid form providing one of the signature elements of this well-loved style. The Arts and Crafts movement that became popular towards the end of the century was originally created as a reaction against Victoriana, although the two styles are strongly linked. The Arts and Crafts look, however, is much simpler; replacing curves and superfluous decoration were fine craftsmanship, integrity of materials and fitness for purpose. Natural wood, waxed rather than polished, copper or cast iron hinges and handles, and textiles printed, woven or embroidered with strictly naturalistic forms are typical features.

RETRO MODE

From the more recent past, there are several distinctive looks to choose from. Art Deco, developed during the 1920s, was the first machine-age style and the first to combine applied art with mass production. Inspired by the ancient Egyptian, Aztec

and Native American cultures, as well as the revolutionary Cubist movement in painting, Deco furnishings rely heavily on graphic forms such as circles, zigzags, triangles, steps and curves. Large areas of neutral colour are combined with pure, vivid hues or muted pastels such as peach or pale green. Signature elements are modern materials like plywood, Bakelite, chrome and tinted glass, with stylized motifs such as sunbursts, female nudes and leaping deer applied as decoration.

During the last half of the twentieth century, certain styles tended to be associated with decades. Since these styles involve fewer formal conventions than their historical equivalents, several provide perfect source material for affectionate and witty recreation. The first era that lends itself readily to this treatment is the 1950s,

Above: Here, the wall hanging, pile rug and animal-print upholstery form a wacky mélange of 1950s prints. The moulded plastic coffee table and telephone, however, are pure 1960s.

Opposite: The natural forms and colours of the Arts and Crafts movement dominate Leicester, a wallpaper by Morris's disciple, John Henry Dearle (above) and Pomegranate, a William Morris fabric (below).

characterized by abstracted geometric and organic shapes (interpreted in a wide range of domestic designs ranging from tables and chairs to textiles, ceramics and lighting), furniture with splayed legs, the widespread use of plastic and laminate surfaces, and a very distinctive use of colour, with favourite shades like bright pink and lime, and subtler ones, like purple, grey and dark red, often combined with black.

In the 1960s dominant decorative influences were youthful and bold like psychedelia, with its vibrant colours and swirling shapes, and Pop Art, which turned commercial images and popular personalities into cultural and artistic icons. As interpreted by the free-spirited hippie movement., the colours and crafts of the Indian subcontinent became part of the design vocabulary and the moon landing inspired all manner of domestic objects with space-age forms and detailing. Although the stunning innovation and creativity associated with the 1960s was bound to level off once the next decade got underway (indeed, the 1970s is often known with some justification as 'the decade that style forgot'), a number of quintessential 1970s objects often appear in fashionably funky interiors, usually as elements of visual irony or kitsch: blobby lava lamps, for instance, and huge, supergraphic murals.

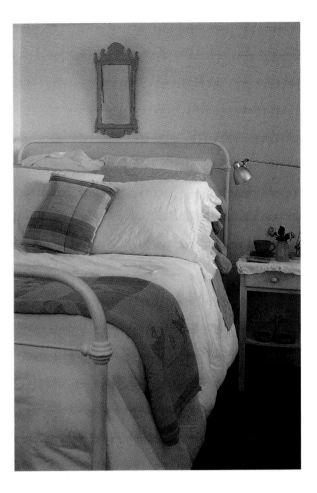

country style

An authentic country look is much less self-conscious than any modern or period scheme. Indeed, rural homes of all kinds are seldom 'designed' in the accepted sense. Their contents have been assembled gradually over the years, each element passed through generations or chosen because it is hardwearing, easy-to-clean and eminently suited for its function. Materials are natural (wood, stone, cotton and rush, for example) and colours echo those found in nature. Furnishings are free of sophisticated embellishment and many of them are handcrafted. The essence of country charm, and one of its defining characteristics, is honesty, so bear in mind that displaying a row of battered farm implements on the wall of a high-rise apartment does not constitute a suitable expression of country style. There are a number of popular variations on the country look: some reflect the affluence of wealthy landowners, while others are associated with a humbler, more modest way of life.

RURAL PROSPERITY

One of the most popular variations on this theme is the classic English country house look, with its acres of floral chintz, patterned wallpaper, massive and highly polished items of furniture, oriental carpets and somewhat elaborate arrangements of photographs, ornaments and memorabilia. Similarly timeless and appealing is the American colonial idiom that combines the elegant European traditions of the first settlers who created it, with the beauty of indigenous materials and local crafts. Signature elements are floors and furnishings made from maple, cherry, hickory and elm, and colours inspired by the New England landscape, such as soft, greyish greens and blues, dark reds and russets and subtle, mustardy yellows. Stencilled motifs, patchwork quilts, needlework samplers and primitive paintings all form an intrinsic part of this look.

Another source of inspiration for those who are particularly drawn to pastoral elegance is the provençal style of southern France, characterized by stone or plaster walls, deep, rich colours like gold, rose and lavender, ceramic tiles, imposing items of furniture (in particular, the armoire or storage cupboard); and the distinctive printed fabric produced in the region, which carries its name. The country dwellings of the Tuscan countryside in Italy share many of these elements, but they are slightly more formal. Typical features are rich textiles, decorative ironwork and the widespread use of terracotta tiles on floors, walls and work surfaces, as well as large pots of flowers, fruit and herbs, also made from terracotta, the area's indigenous clay. Colours are faded and painted floral arrangements and landscapes adorn both the walls and the furniture.

One look that has gained hugely in popularity over recent years is associated with a very different kind of countryside: that of Sweden. Unusually, its visual personality did not

evolve organically, but was created deliberately by late nineteenth-century artists Carl and Karin Larsson to suit both the forbidding landscape and their life with a young family. Their house had a conventional timber structure, but the imaginative decorations they added stamped it indelibly with their personalities. Because sunlight was sparse and watery, it was highly valued, so windows in Larsson-style country houses are left unadorned, fitted with shutters or dressed with lengths of filmy lace or lawn. Wooden floorboards, furniture (elegant antiques or simple, rustic pieces) and architectural detailing are painted in soft pastels or clear, bright colours, while walls are plainly plastered or perhaps covered with tongue-and-groove cladding, then painted. Key accessories are trailing plants, striped cotton rugs, stencilled motifs on walls and furniture, and lightweight, informal fabrics such as checks and stripes (see page 215).

PEASANT PERSPECTIVES

Whatever regional or national characteristics they reflect, this group of styles are all linked with a basic, relatively harsh, rural existence that is heavily dependent on nature and unrelieved by luxury or ornamentation. Almost universally, walls are a soft, creamy white, floors are made of stone or wood, and furniture is practical and plain. In a classic English country-cottage scheme, the walls are plastered or lined with simple wooden panelling. All the timber – on the floors and in the furniture – is painted or stripped and waxed rather than stained and varnished to a high-gloss finish. Low-slung beams may be discoloured with smoke from the open fire, but they should never be painted black. Short curtains made from homespun cotton or linen, either unpatterned or woven with a traditional stripe or check, hang from iron, brass or wooden rails. All the objects displayed (graceful jugs, sturdy baskets, handmade rugs and thick candles) serve a useful purpose.

Transposed to the New World, this necessary and unself-conscious practicality was woven into the doctrine of a small New England religious sect known as the Shakers. Their austere and beautiful rooms are simply furnished and contain only pieces that are exquisitely made, completely unadorned and perfectly fit for their purpose – often with surprisingly modern features such as small wheels and collapsible frames. Fitted storage cupboards accommodate a variety of objects in purpose-designed compartments, hiding all clutter from view, while short, homespun curtains provide a softening touch.

In the same way that certain decorating traditions tend to be common to areas with a temperate climate and landscape, country homes in warmer regions share several distinctive features like bold colour, primitive patterns and large expanses of cool stone, tiling and rough plaster. The desert region of the south-western part of the USA, for example, inspired the unpretentious Santa Fé style, a striking blend of the cultural traditions of the colonists who settled in nearby Mexico and the native tribes of the surrounding regions. Typical

Above: All Shaker furnishings are supremely practical. When they're not in use, as many items as possible are hung on turned pegs projecting from a slender timber rail fixed around the room at shoulder height or above.

Opposite: The unmistakably Mediterranean atmosphere of Provence or Tuscany permeates this simple kitchen, from the plain plaster walls and wooden surfaces to signature touches like woven wicker, hand-thrown pottery and fragrant herbs in a natural terracotta pot.

Santa Fé-style rooms have fittings and furnishings that are crudely made from local timber – the dark, heavy, carved wood common to Spanish-speaking countries. Textiles are handwoven in earthy hues of burnt orange, brick red, rich brown and black. Windows and doors are closed and covered with shutters or drapes to keep out both the dust and the enervating heat. In place of creamy earthenware and polished brass, there is wrought iron, terracotta and pierced tin.

In its tropical incarnation reminiscent of places like Greece and the Caribbean, this look is defined by pure, vivid shades of yellow, pink, green and blue. Rooms are light and airy, and they are often arranged in an open-plan style, with crisp, cotton curtains at the windows and filmy netting around the beds. Decorative details include peasant embroidery, painted pottery and cheerful displays of locally grown fruit, flowers, grasses and vegetables.

exotic style

While most of us want our surroundings to reflect familiar design conventions, others long to experiment with schemes inspired by very different ways of life. If you are excited by the idea of using space, light, colour and even furnishings in completely new ways, widen the range of design traditions you are prepared to consider. Adventurous souls who travel extensively are likely to have acquired a collection of textiles and craft objects that can create stunning visual effects in the context of a sympathetic scheme.

JAPANESE TRANQUILLITY

Spare and cool, the oriental look suits those who value order and serenity above luxury and ornament. Rooms are large, with plain white walls, simply framed windows and low furniture. Colours are light and neutral, with small areas of contrasting black, lacquer red and deep yellow. Woven mats and flat cushions accommodate the tradition

Opposite: Lacquer red, a favourite accent colour in conventional oriental schemes, takes the lead in this small but dramatic bedroom.

Below: Dark wood, brass, papier mâché, woven matting and rich, handwoven textiles suggest a look inspired by Asian culture.

mixing & matching

Combining favourite pieces of furniture and design elements from different disciplines can either produce unique and stylish rooms or lead to decorating disaster. Keep in mind the essential spirit and atmosphere of the looks you want to marry; those borne out of austerity or a doctrine of simplicity are unlikely to complement those celebrating detail and ornament. So rustic oak looks great in Arts and Crafts-inspired rooms or classic modern ones, but sits uncomfortably beside neoclassical or Victorian designs. The stark simplicity of oriental pottery might work well in a country room, but the effect would be lost in a formal, chintzy one. When you're going for a bold mix of idioms, keep the background (wall, floors and windows) unobtrusive. A few unifying elements (cream lamps or tablecloths, maybe) will also unify a scheme, but avoid crowding the various elements together or your careful blend of shapes and colours will resemble an unruly muddle.

of sleeping, sitting and taking meals on the floor, and translucent paper screens divide the space, conceal parts of the room when necessary and provide privacy at the windows. Curtains would not suit a Japanese-style room, but simple shutters or blinds complement the look very well. The few objects on display are beautifully made and pure of line; collections of twigs or a tiny, perfect bonsai tree add a natural touch.

ASIAN RICHNESS

Although there is no single decorating style associated with the Indian subcontinent, the various countries and cultures within it all make beautiful, affordable textiles and handicrafts for worldwide export. Experiment by setting these things off against rich colours and mixing them with sympathetic items acquired locally. Plain surfaces work best: try painting walls in deep saffron, ochre, dark rose or subtle aqua. Match the woodwork to the walls or choose another shade of equal intensity such as mellow cream, but avoid the harshness of bright white. Lay flat-woven rugs, such as druggets, dhurries or kelims, on the floor, hang them on walls or drape them over tables, beds or sofas. For fabrics, choose from plain, slubby cotton (woven in lots of gorgeous colours) or embroidered Kashmiri crewelwork, and try to find ways of displaying exquisite saris.

THE LURE OF THE CASBAH

Decorating schemes inspired by the cultures of northern Africa also involve imaginative interpretation rather than precise recreation Those influenced by Morocco, Algeria and Tunisia rely heavily on opulent textiles, richly layered, often on deep, low daybeds piled with cushions or huge ottomans. Signature colours are jewel-like and displayed extravagantly in the form of coloured pottery, glass and mosaic tiles on tabletops, floors and walls. Traces of Moorish influence remain in the form of graceful arches, complex inlay on furniture and small objects, tooled leatherwork and carved, folding screens.

THE MAGIC
OF COLOUR

For many people, the prospect of using colour freely and boldly is too intimidating to contemplate. Yet colour is not only the most dynamic element in any design scheme, it is also one of the cheapest to use and the easiest to change if you're not happy with the result. Once you discover the seductive power of colour and the thrilling possibilities it opens up, you'll never look back. With the sweep of a paintbrush, colour can alter the entire personality of your rooms, change apparent shapes and sizes, and transform a collection of seemingly disparate architectural features and furnishing items into a sleek, cohesive style statement. Certain shades, too, have complex psychological associations that may subliminally influence your perception of temperature and can even affect your mood.

tricks of the eye

One of the most familiar of all decorating dictums is the rule that pale colours make a room look bigger, while darker ones reduce its perceived size. While this is certainly true, it's worth bearing in mind that there are other ways of achieving similar results. One of the most successful tactics is to choose the same colour treatment for walls, ceiling and woodwork: this kind of visual simplification not only makes a room feel more spacious, it also disguises any awkward shapes and ugly features. Use the same device to make a huge, but infinitely practical chest of drawers or cupboard less obtrusive by painting it to match the walls. Similarly, choosing white to make a ceiling appear higher is seldom necessary and often counter productive since a dramatic change in tone between ceiling and wall accentuates, rather than disguises, any proportional inadequacies. As a general rule, the closer in tone all the surfaces and furnishing elements are to each other, the more spacious a room will seem. This doesn't mean that everything has to be the same colour, but if enhancing the impression of space is your top priority, then cameo pink walls with a matching ceiling combined with, say, natural flooring, furniture made from blond wood and rich, creamy curtains would be more successful than the extreme contrasts of dark, stained floorboards, white walls and multi-hued furnishings. It's important, though, to avoid becoming obsessed with this concept; after all, making rooms appear a little bit bigger or higher is much less important than creating an attractive and inviting home.

changing moods

Whatever your personal preferences, each colour has its own specific qualities that affect everyone. Strong, bright tones are naturally much more potent than light, chalky ones. Soft, subtle versions of green, blue, mauve, pink and apricot are tranquil and soothing shades: use them for living areas, bedrooms and bathrooms. Sunny yellow, rich red, deep rose, burnt orange and baked terracotta, on the other hand, have a strongly energizing effect. These colours are well suited to areas such as dining rooms and hallways, which are not used for relaxation, and where people tend not to linger for extended periods. For kitchens and workrooms, look for middle-range tones that cheer and stimulate without overpowering the senses.

In many cases, the particular shade you choose is more important than the basic colour. Ochre-based banana yellow, for instance, adds a flattering glow to even the smallest, darkest space and lifts the spirits immediately, while a lemony tint is apt to take on a greenish cast whenever the sun disappears, and it is very unsettling to live with in large quantities. In the same way, pale aqua and watery eau de nil are calming and easy on the eye, whereas grey-tinged shades such as airforce blue and pea green can feel chilly and unwelcoming in both temperature and mood, and large expanses of brighter shades like cobalt blue and grass green are more likely to induce headaches than alleviate tension.

colour harmony

Aim to think in terms of colour groups instead of basing your choices on the more traditional concept of the colour wheel, or trying to match individual tones precisely. On the whole, colours of the same intensity and type work well together: tender pastels, 1950s dayglo shades, dusty earth tones, clear primaries and gaudy pinks and oranges. Some of the most common decorating failures result from a dramatic imbalance among the dominant colours: some shades are dark, vivid or muddy, while others are light and clear. A sofa covered in deep saffron, for example, will sit uncomfortably against an anaemic off-white or baby-blue wall. To complement its intensity, choose a background shade of similar visual weight, such as Tuscan pink or watery aquamarine.

Relieve large expanses of strong colour with neutral shades, but again, be selective in your choice. White is perfect with pastels, fresh seaside shades and clear primaries, but it will draw away all the richness from more mellow and subtle tones. So, if the main elements of your scheme are lavender, sage and mustard or topaz, sapphire and ruby red, set them off against natural materials such as wood, cane and coir, and surfaces painted in dairy cream, French beige or soft buff. You can also make use of the strong affinity between colours of the same type to link otherwise unrelated decorating elements. The haphazard jumble of family cast-offs, junk-store finds and cheap, modern pieces that most people start out with will suddenly appear stylish and modern when you paint them all in contemporary sherbet pastels or gaudy citrus brights.

solid ground

In the end, the only appropriate basis for choosing a colour is that you feel good about it and it suits your home and the way you live. All too often, though, inexperience leaves the first-time decorator vulnerable to unwholesome influences. Of these, the most prevalent are fashion and cowardice. Like

decorating styles, fashionable colours change from year to year and keeping up with every new furnishing trend can be considerably more costly than updating your wardrobe. It's also true that the relentless pursuit of novelty sometimes throws the spotlight on shades that are as impractical and unflattering as they are unusual. Perhaps the most widespread of all incentives for choosing room colours, however, is timidity. Although the past few years have seen an encouraging burst of enthusiasm for colour, millions of walls are still being painted white or off-white because they're regarded as 'safe' and they 'go with everything'. There's no doubt that decorating palettes based on pale, neutral tints can look stunning, but only when the choice is a positive and informed one, not a design cop-out. Keep in mind, too, that pure white walls are best suited to parts of the world where natural light is abundant. In more temperate climes (and darkish rooms) they tend to take on a grey and dingy cast. To increase the impression of light, choose soft white with a hint of pink, yellow or apricot, or be brave and opt for a full-blooded version of one of these warmer hues. And unless you're prepared for the harsh glare of chemical brighteners, steer clear of any tin marked 'brilliant' white.

Another common misconception is that monochrome schemes (those based on shades of one colour) are an easy option: they're not. Throwing together a range of greens, for example, creates aesthetic mayhem when deep olive, fresh lettuce, cool aquamarine, pale mint and bright viridian are all involved. Even the trusted neutrals present similar pitfalls. Cream, for example, is available in hundreds of variations – some cool, some warm, some clear, some muted. Sticking with groups of different, but naturally sympathetic colours is much more likely to be a success.

tests & trials

Not surprisingly, large areas of colour – walls, floors, curtains and upholstery – tend to inspire the most anxiety, which is perfectly understandable, since mistakes on this scale are not only difficult to ignore, but also very expensive. Before you commit yourself to any of these major elements, try to get hold of decent-sized samples of all the options so you can see them in situ. When it comes to paint, postage-stamp sized squares on a colour card will not do the job. Most manufacturers sell sample pots of all their standard colours. Buy one of each shade you're considering, brush the colours onto separate strips of plain lining paper and pin them to the wall. If your favourite shades need to be specially mixed, don't hesitate to pay for a small tin of each one. Similarly, the swatches of carpet and furnishing fabric that most stores give away are of very little practical use, but many suppliers will let you have more generous samples – especially of carpet – if you leave a small, returnable deposit. Again, if small fabric cuttings are all that's on offer, invest in lengths of two or three metres that you can tuck over a curtain rail or drape across a chair. When your samples are in place, leave them there for a week or two so that you can see how each one looks throughout the day, and in different lights. You will find that living with the alternatives over a period of time leads you almost unconsciously towards your final choice.

ROOMS FOR LIVING

Particularly with your first home, it's all too easy to get carried away with decorating fantasies that are actually very difficult to live with from day to day. Especially seductive is the perfect calm and ultimate chic of a very pale colour scheme. Those who have an inherently ordered and fastidious nature (and friends who share these admirable traits) may suit this look very well. For most of us, however, the dream is likely to fade away very quickly when, inevitably, everyday grime and occasional spills begin to sully the pale purity, and maintaining the immaculate surfaces threatens to become an unhealthy obsession.

Opposite: Deep, jewel-like hues have a natural affinity with one another that you can count on to produce a successful scheme.

Left: Dark wood and burnished brass set off the rich, warm reds that dominate this seductive dining chamber. In a room like this, giving the skirting board a coat of snowy gloss would be like wearing shiny white shoes with a velvet ballgown.

USING PATTERN

Like colour, pattern tends to intimidate those who are not used to working with it. For creating interest, depth and sheer visual richness, however, there are few design tools more potent. If you are equally tempted and dismayed by the possibilities on offer, there are two main tactics you can employ to reduce the risk of failure: either choose all your patterns from a range of coordinated fabrics, wallpapers and accessories, or begin in a low-key way with one or two small areas of pattern, then add more as your confidence and style sense develop. The first option is certainly the safest one, but the result often has a sterile, showroomy feel and inevitably lacks the originality and sparkle of a scheme that you have sourced and put together yourself.

guidelines for success

Also in common with colour, patterns can grouped according to type: formal and elegant, cheerful and cosy, bold and graphic, opulent and exotic, or simple and fresh. To put together a successful mix, choose several examples with a similar feeling: classic gingham checks and artless country florals, for example, rich paisley weaves and oriental rugs, African motifs and modern geometric shapes, or period stripes and traditional chintzes.

When you're using fabric and wallpaper samples to experiment with different combinations, you'll get a much more accurate idea of how they'll look if you approximate the comparative size of each one to its intended purpose in the finished room. If, for example, you are looking at a collection of patterns – some for the wallpaper, some for the sofa and some for throw cushions – arranging sizable lengths of paper with medium-sized squares of sofa fabric and small swatches of cushion material will give you a much clearer idea of the final effect than playing with same-size cuttings of all the designs under consideration.

To display a collection of different patterns to their best advantage and provide much-needed visual relief, be sure to balance them with large areas of solid colour. Remember, too, when you're at the planning stage, to take into account the impact of dominant features in the room that you may not immediately think of as patterned: rows of books with multi-coloured spines, for instance, a desk covered with family photographs, shelves crowded with china or decorative glass or a dressing-table surface with bright bottles, jars, tubes and boxes of every description on permanent display.

illusion & artifice

As long as the colours and moods of your patterns work well together, they needn't all be the same size. Keep a close eye, though, on the relationship between the size of a pattern and the proportions of your room. Big patterns

This simple roll-up blind is lined with a traditional woven check that blends perfectly with its fresh floral motif printed on white linen. Both patterns, and the way they're combined, suggest a Swedish influence.

are usually intended for larger rooms, so they can easily overpower more modest ones. Similarly, when viewed across a cavernous expanse of space, the detailing and rhythm of a tiny pattern will disappear completely.

Vertical stripes increase the impression of height, so when you want to make a room appear taller, paint or paper the walls accordingly. Unless your walls are very straight and even, though, subtle, painted stripes with appealingly wobbly edges are a wiser choice than wallpaper with bright, graphic lines, which will highlight any flaws.

When it comes to camouflaging clumsy architectural features like steeply sloping ceilings and projecting corners, an all-over pattern is even more effective than a single-colour treatment. Achieve this result by covering both walls and ceiling with the same paper (choose a small pattern to avoid awkward joins), or pull problem features together with a subtle paint effect such as colourwashing or sponging. Alternatively, if you have the patience and the skill, apply a repeat motif drawn by hand, such as simple spots, crosses or squiggles, or use a stencil or rubber stamp.

Above and left: Mixing patterns that share the same general mood and intensity of colour creates a harmonious effect even when the hues involved are surprisingly contrasting and vivid. Keep in mind that cheerful printed wallpapers tend to work best when used with large areas of painted, polished or waxed wood and natural materials like cane.

Opposite: Here, the same principles have been employed to combine three different fabrics (two sophisticated checks and one exotic paisley). In this room, the signature style is traditional, yet reinterpreted with a contemporary twist.

THE REALM OF THE SENSES

Creating a home involves much more than simply putting together a collection of stylish decorating schemes; it also means surrounding yourself with materials, fragrances and sounds that soothe your senses and refresh your spirits. Once you've decided on the dominant atmosphere you want for your environment, explore all the subtle, sensual touches you can add to reinforce it.

texture

Making the best possible use of the texture in your rooms does not necessarily mean installing bare brick walls, fake fur rugs or satin sheets. Used skilfully, texture can add interest, depth and sensuality in a vast range of understated, yet very powerful ways. To strengthen a scheme based on natural materials and hues, look for wooden furniture that has been waxed and polished to a deep, satin-like patina, wool fabrics and carpets with a thick, knobbly weave and crisp, waffle-weave cotton, coarse linen and raw silk. Make shelves from chunky, weathered railway sleepers or other reclaimed wood and display pieces of sculptural driftwood and unusual stones together in groups.

For a cosier feeling, choose pile-weave fabrics like cotton velvet and chenille for your chairs and sofa, and drape them with cuddly blankets and throws. Cut up old sweaters to make tactile cushions (or turn them out yourself with jumbo needles or crochet hooks and buttery, soft wool) and place a furry rug beside your bed to tickle your toes. Add a touch of sensuality to formal rooms with finely figured silk and brocade trimmed with fringes and tassels that beg to be fondled, ornaments of burnished brass and polished silver, and mirror-finish mahogany or rosewood surfaces.

Below and right: The feel of a surface against your skin can be just as important as the way it looks. For maximum tactile stimulation, mix (from left to right) crisp cotton, soft wool, plump, cushiony quilting and subtly textured leather.

Cool, sophisticated decorating schemes provide the ideal backdrop for suede and leather – either in self-indulgent expanses on a sofa or armchair, or as tasteful accessories such as cushions, photograph albums and wastepaper baskets. Real skins are costly, of course, and – some would argue – morally unacceptable, but modern technology has produced a range of astonishing fakes that are virtually indistinguishable from the real thing – to the touch as well as to the eye. Plain fabrics, lightly padded and quilted in graphic diamonds or squares, provide an ingenious combination of design purity and textural richness. Add rough, hand-thrown pottery and surfaces of polished marble, cool glass, brushed steel and watery zinc.

In contemporary rooms that tend towards the quirky or exotic, indulge both your imagination and your sensuality by making full use of fake fur – not just in the form of cushions, but draped across a bed, thrown over a sofa or used as a cover for a large table. For the widest choice, check out dressmaking materials, as well as those intended for furnishings. Collect Indian textiles with their intricate,

hand-stitched motifs, and set them off against the rich texture of culturally coordinated fabrics such as slubbed cotton and embroidered crewelwork.

As well as extending your design skills, an awareness of texture can also be useful in a number of practical ways. If you have smoothly plastered walls, for example, apply emulsion paint with an eggshell sheen to gently reflect and enhance the effect of any available light, whether natural or artificial. Even the subtlest shine will highlight every crack, bump and hole, though, so if camouflage is your aim, choose a matt finish instead and apply it in the form of an almost imperceptible colourwash or sponge effect.

fragrance

To add a delightfully sensual element to your domestic environment and increase your sense of well-being at the same time, fill your rooms with subtle fragrance. If you enjoy tending houseplants, choose species like lilies or hyacinths that produce an intoxicating scent as they bloom, or search out other varieties, such as scented-leaf geraniums, whose

Above and opposite: Experiment with different ways to subtly perfume your rooms. For the ultimate in floral luxury, treat yourself to the powerful fragrance of fresh roses, lilacs, sweet peas, lilies or stocks. For a more lasting essence, or one with warmer, spicier or more complex notes, choose delicious scented candles.

smell, though less powerful, lasts for much longer. Alternatively, arrange large, open containers (bowls, baskets, tins or boxes) of potpourri wherever you can find room or substitute handfuls of dried lavender, rose petals or herbs. Hang fragrant pomanders (store-bought or homemade) near the front door to give you a lift when you come home tired and stressed. At night, use scented candles to perfume the air, but never leave them burning when you're not in the room. For an instant burst of a favourite scent, try one of the new, upmarket room sprays that come in a range of scrumptious, emotionally appealing flavours redolent of home baking, spicy fruit and damp earth.

If you want to employ fragrance in a more focussed way, infuse the air with one of the essential oils used in aromatherapy. There are several ways to do this. You can either warm some oil in a special burner or vaporizer, place a few drops inside a special light-bulb ring or directly on the bulb, or add some oil to a small container of water placed next to a radiator or other heat source. Any store that sells these oils should also provide information about how each one should be used: lavender and rose, for example, are calming and relaxing, while citrus oils, such as lemon and lime, are refreshing and stimulating. Be sure to ask for advice and follow it closely since essential oils are very powerful and some can even be dangerous if they're ingested or applied directly onto the skin.

sound

If one of your first responses to joy, anxiety or depression is to lose yourself in music, you may be able to use this sensitivity to sound in less obvious ways. For example, many people find the gurgle of running water calming, but few properties boast their own babbling brook, so consider installing an electric fountain outside (in the garden, or on a terrace or balcony), or in a corner of your living room. Hang tinkling wind chimes near a door to catch the breeze and encourage birds to sing outside your windows by regularly putting out food and water for them.

3
elements of
decoration

Every decision you make in terms of decorating and furnishing should be inspired by your personal vision – how you would like your first home to look, what kind of social, leisure and work activities you want it to accommodate, and even the length of time you intend to stay there. Knowing what you want is not enough, though: you can't turn your dreams into reality until you realize exactly which tasks you face, what your options are, and how the decisions you make are likely to affect you.

THE WHOLE PICTURE

With so many exciting design opportunities on offer, it's tempting to use as many of them as possible in your first home. Certainly, choosing a completely different scheme for every part of it may at first seem an ingenious way of accommodating all the different looks, colours and materials you've set your heart on, but it's important to realize that the rooms you live in are not separate, closed-off boxes; they are all part of a single interior landscape where each space flows directly into the next. While there's no need for all your rooms to look exactly the same, their dominant styles and colours should have some kind of visual unity to avoid any abrupt and unsettling changes of mood: a fresh, funky entrance hall done out in pure, intense colours and shiny surfaces, for instance, should not lead into an elegant period living area, or a bedroom full of tender pastel hues and sensual textures. When you feel torn between two obviously incompatible looks, it's a much better idea to commit yourself fully to one of them and to save the other scheme for next time.

visual links

As well as harmonizing the basic mood of all your schemes, try to provide several linking elements between them: laying the same (or at least the same colour) floor covering throughout is one of the most effective of all design tactics both for enhancing visual cohesion and increasing the impression of space. (Awkward joins between different floor coverings at the entrance to a room, on the other hand, always look dowdy and untidy.) So, if your taste runs to neutral tones, choose pale timber or honey-coloured tiles for the kitchen and bathroom, and natural coir, sisal or carpet in the same shade for the living room, bedroom and hall. Or indulge a preference for bright colours by fitting lino or vinyl where you need a waterproof surface, then echoing your chosen shade with plain carpet everywhere else.

Another subtle way to pull your schemes together is by matching all the woodwork: skirting boards, architraves, internal doors and door and window frames. As with floors, go for a traditional neutral, like soft white or buff, or experiment with a stronger colour that ties in with your overall theme. To further extend the visual dimensions of every room, paint all the skirting boards in the same colour as the adjacent floor coverings.

Right: Warm tones and natural materials form a cohesive link between rooms. Here, jungle prints, carved wood and towering twig sculptures all hint at exotic tropical influences.

If your heating system depends on ugly metal radiators, make them less obtrusive by painting them all to blend with the adjoining walls. To do this, first treat each one with an acrylic primer, then give it a coat of ordinary emulsion paint in your chosen colour. Radiators next to painted wood panelling need only a standard undercoating, then a coat of whatever eggshell or silk finish you've used on the timber. Alternatively, choose the same stylish camouflage treatment for all of them: a simple wooden grille, perhaps, or a cover made from wire mesh, woven cane or cheap garden trellis.

While every home should have one or two basic elements that are common to each room, the extent to which you extend this premise is very much a matter of personal preference. Window treatments (or just curtain rails), door furniture and fitted storage units are all possible candidates for similar theming.

Below: Throughout this uniformly cool, pale house, the walls and woodwork are soft white, the radiators are hidden behind clever cut-out panels, and the floors are natural. Some, like the one in this Swedish-flavoured guest bedroom, have been fitted with coir matting, while others are laid with blond boards.

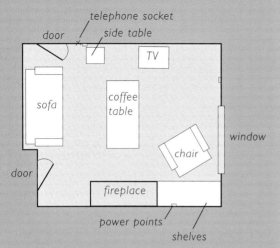

Above: Badly planned rooms can be dangerous and inconvenient. Here, one door can't open fully, the chair and sofa are too far apart for easy communication, and the seating area has a limited view of the TV. Only one seat can be reached from the phone, and then only if the cable is trailed across the doorway. The table is too far from the sofa and the easy chair is in a draught.

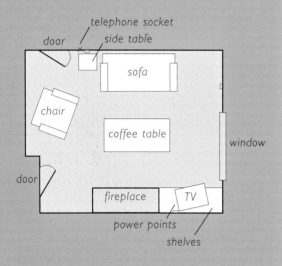

Above: In this much more successful plan, traffic paths are wide and unimpeded by wires or flexes, doors can open freely and every item of furniture is accessible. The main seating area is arranged so people can watch TV, chat on the phone or converse, with a centrally placed surface close at hand for drinks and snacks.

scale plans

Detailed floor plans on which you can experiment with different arrangements of furniture will never completely do away with the more hands-on trial-and-error approach to organizing rooms, but they're an excellent place to start off from. Measure every room in your home accurately and draw a scale plan of it on a large sheet of graph paper. Mark out all the windows and doors, remembering to include the amount of clearance required by any that open into the room. Note the distance between the bottom of each window and the floor so you know which items will fit directly underneath it. Add the position of all the radiators, power and telecommunications points, wall lights and permanent features such as fireplaces or built-in shelves and plumbing facilities, where relevant. Then, using the same scale, cut out shapes from graph paper to represent every piece of furniture you own and those you are planning to buy for the foreseeable future.

Begin by positioning all the major items – bed, sofa, dining table – since there will probably be a limited number of places in which they can fit, then play around with the smaller bits and pieces. Always take into account the extra space you'll need to get in and out of dining chairs comfortably, say, to open a cupboard door or to pull out the drawers of a filing cabinet, or even to stretch out your legs in front of an armchair. The purpose of this exercise is to provide all the core information you need (such as whether each piece of furniture fits into the space you have in mind for it, or is likely to interfere with any of its neighbours) before any aesthetic considerations come into play.

What floor plans can't do, however, is give you an exact picture of how the finished room will look: how the various shapes and proportions work together, the way one particular surface relates to another one nearby and whether the reflected light from a mirror will cause an annoying glare across the screen of your television or computer. Sometimes, apparently ideal floor plans fall down after several weeks of daily use because the sharp edge of a coffee or side table projects into a heavily used traffic path, for example, or you discover there isn't a suitable surface for placing drinks or stacking magazines anywhere near your favourite chair.

ESTABLISHING PRIORITIES

When you're faced with a bewildering collection of tasks to accomplish and things to buy, combined with limited funds to work with, it's easy to allow impulse, ignorance and impatience to take over. Whether you find the prospect of creating a home unbearably exciting or inconvenient and tedious, making instant, easy choices is the wrong way to go about it since this approach only lands you with a random, incomplete and unsuitable assortment of decorations and furnishings.

first & foremost

However heartbreaking you find it to invest large amounts of cash behind the scenes, always take care of fundamentals such as heating, plumbing and insulation before you do anything else, since you'll never feel at home when your rooms are chilly and your hot water system unreliable. In the long term, of course, sound, efficient services pay for themselves quickly (and ultimately free up much more of your budget) since faulty and inefficient ones are wasteful and costly to operate.

Another very basic priority – and the single most important piece of furniture in your home – is your bed, so don't be tempted to compromise here. It's important, too, to make this one of your first purchases since sleeping soundly and waking refreshed will help you cope with any domestic discomforts, frustrations and inconveniences that may crop up along the way. Early on, too, replace old, stained bathroom fittings and tiles with clean, new ones. In both cases, the most basic versions (usually plain white) are inexpensive and the huge practical and aesthetic difference they make will lift your spirits magically. If necessary, leave extras like a separate shower until later on. Similarly, make sure the kitchen sink and taps are in good condition and install basic appliances, such as the fridge, cooker, washing machine and any small gadgets you can't live without, as soon as possible. Save money by searching for discontinued models or slightly shop-soiled ones, but for safety reasons, never use second-hand electrical goods – even those donated by well-meaning friends and relations – unless they are fully reconditioned and guaranteed. To reduce labour costs (and take advantage of quantity discounts on materials), try to arrange for all jobs of one kind, such as plumbing, electrics or carpentry, to be done at the same time.

Sometimes, the degree to which a particular furnishing element can transform your environment earns it a place near the top of your priority list. Even when your rooms are almost empty, for example, laying good-quality carpet and thick underlay throughout will increase their visual (and actual) warmth considerably and give an increased impression of space and a finished, pulled-together look. It also provides excellent sound insulation and makes the whole flat or house

more welcoming and user-friendly by turning the floor into a potential seating area. Even if your preference is for a hard surface, such as floorboards rather than carpet, the potential benefits in terms of style, visual cohesion and perceived space are enormous.

Another super-value design tool is lighting. If the only fittings you have are central ceiling pendants, you can alter the look and mood of your rooms dramatically by investing in appropriate table, floor or wall lamps for everyday use. What's more, the right lighting will make it much easier for you to see what you're doing in work areas such as the kitchen and home office.

make do & mend

In order to have funds available for your top-priority projects, you will probably have to make savings elsewhere and one of the most sensible places to start is at your windows. Here, the range of potential treatments is infinite, the scope for using your imagination limitless, but the expense terrifying. But at this stage, your only pressing need is for something that protects your privacy and looks fairly smart; in the bedroom you may also want to keep out the early morning sun. So, if you find your funds are depleting quickly, hang inexpensive curtains or blinds, or explore more unusual options, such as positioning a hinged screen in front of the bedroom window, or applying adhesive sheets of translucent plastic to the glass in the bathroom.

Tables of every description are another furnishing requisite on which ingenuity and artifice can work wonders. You should have at least one large table for dining and working on, and several smaller ones – beside your bed, for example, and near the sofa. However battered or hideous they may seem, as long as they are basically sturdy and the right size and height for their purpose, they can usually be camouflaged, brightened up or revamped at very little cost. Simply adding a fresh coat of paint or stripping away the old one is sometimes all that's needed. If you're feeling creative, tile the top of an old table or have a sheet of glass cut to fit and arrange a collection of postcards or photographs underneath it. Whatever room it's in, even a table with no redeeming features at all can look fantastic when you hide it underneath a sensational cover: a

Opposite: Cut costs and preserve privacy by covering the panes in your bathroom window with translucent film. Here, the stark whiteness is relieved by random cut-outs in the form of chubby numerals.

Right: To turn a homely old table into the focus of a candy-bright colour scheme, drape it with a shiny cloth of PVC-covered cotton in a flowery retro print. Echo the dominant hues in a pretty bead curtain.

Below: Any piece of upholstered furniture that is nicely proportioned and in good condition can be transformed with a loose cover. The slubby whiteness of this example in plain linen is set off with a fluffy woollen, chocolate-coloured throw.

beautiful quilt, maybe, or a sheet, a huge throw or a length of felt, which you can buy in a spectacular variety of colours from companies who supply the display and exhibition trades.

Storage, too, although absolutely vital in terms of both the appearance and the smooth operation of your home, need not consume too much of your start-up budget since there are plenty of clever, stylish and low-cost solutions to choose from, in the form of both ready-made furniture and improvised shelves, hooks, baskets, racks and boxes.

cover & conceal

Comfortable seating is an essential component of every home and one that can represent serious expenditure, but here again, ugly sofas and upholstered chairs – if they are sound and supportive – are easy to disguise under a vast throw of some kind. Or, for a slightly bigger outlay, but much less than the cost of new furniture, you could transform them with some new loose covers. When you are faced with the prospect of starting from scratch, try to invest in good-quality seating since it will last – and retain its youthful good looks – much longer than anything at the cheaper end of the market. Dining and occasional chairs, on the other hand, like tables and storage furniture, are relatively easy to buy cheaply or to renovate.

Opposite: This old school desk, unearthed in a junk shop and given an artfully slapdash coat of paint, fulfils a dual function as both dressing and bedside table.

common sense & compromise

In all probability, you may not be able to afford everything you really want for your new home immediately. Inevitably, you will have to wait and compromise, but the areas in which you make these compromises (and the form they take) can represent the difference between disappointment and delight. Fitting cheap floor covering in areas subjected to heavy traffic, for example, is never a good idea. It will wear into ugly, and sometimes dangerous, bald patches very quickly and the cost of replacement, on top of extras such as underlay and fitting, will be far greater than the amount you would have spent on an appropriate quality in the first place.

With most items of furniture, if your first choice is out of your financial reach or nothing seems quite right, it's often tempting to settle for a less expensive version that you tell yourself is just as nice, or to give up and buy a nondescript piece. But while second-best choices, unlike true objects of desire, are more likely to fall out of favour than to grow in your affections over time, they are still too valuable to be cast aside when you feel you need a change.

Consider going to the opposite extreme and improvising completely, or selecting something very cheap on the understanding that you will replace it reasonably quickly. If, for instance, you dream of a designer dining table, then buying a chain-store copy even at half the original price will erode your budget seriously. Instead, opt for a basic folding model from an office supply company or even a builder's trestle table, and save your money until either you can get the one you want, or you perhaps spot something less costly that you like just as much as your initial choice.

Finally, try to make sure your expectations are reasonable. A few items of cheap furniture may be just what you need to add colour and quirky style to your rooms until you can afford to replace them, and this is exactly what they are designed for. If you are counting on them to give lasting service, you are heading for frustration.

WALLS

The walls of any room (with or without the ceiling) represent its largest single surface. They provide the background for all the other furnishing elements that are to be included, and wherever you choose to look, they are smack in your line of vision. Whatever kind of treatment you decide to use here, therefore, will dominate your finished scheme.

Because there are fewer practical limitations on wall finishes than virtually any other surface (you don't walk on them, sit on them or spill drinks on them), your range of appropriate decorative options is uniquely wide and varied. Select from the following types of wall finish:

paint

The easiest, and usually the cheapest and quickest, transformation you can effect in any room is to paint it a different colour. But before you are seduced by any of the enormous number of shades on offer, however, you should familiarize yourself with the main types of paint on the market and decide which ones you want to use where.

However complex and technical any survey of paint types may at first appear, the basic differences between them are straightforward: in composition, every paint is either water- or solvent-based (sometimes known as oil-based). If you're unsure of a particular tin, check the product information on the side. Broadly, these paints have certain characteristics:

Water-based paints (emulsions, acrylic gloss and some primers):

- dry more quickly
- smell less strong
- hold colour better
- can be washed off (and thinned out) with water
- contain fewer toxic chemicals so are less harmful to the environment
- are ideal for matt finishes

But they also:

- wear less well
- mark more easily
- offer less flexibility for beginners when it comes to trying out decorative effects since they dry almost instantly

Solvent-based paints (most gloss, eggshell and enamel finishes, plus undercoats and primers):

- are extremely hard-wearing
- can create a shiny finish
- withstand higher levels of damp and moisture (in bathrooms, kitchens and utility rooms, for example)

But they also:

- dry very slowly
- have a strong chemical smell
- hold colour less effectively (whites tend to yellow)
- must be thinned out and removed with solvent such as white spirit

Within these categories, the main differences between one kind of paint and another tend to involve either the effect they give when dry, their porosity (and therefore their resistance to water), or the durability of finish. The types you are most likely to come across are:

Vinyl matt emulsion

This is the conventional choice for walls and ceilings. Water-based, it is easy to apply, it covers well and the non-reflective finish helps to hide minor surface flaws. However, it also tends to mark fairly easily.

Vinyl silk emulsion

Also water-based, this paint has a slight sheen which makes it slightly more durable than vinyl matt and it is also easier to wipe clean. However, it is more likely to highlight surface lumps and bumps.

Solid emulsion

Available in either vinyl silk or vinyl matt, this is a non-drip paint that is packaged in its own tray. Easy to use, it comes in a limited colour range.

Kitchen/bathroom emulsion

This paint contains fungicide to make it resistant to damp and condensation. It has a soft sheen finish.

One-coat emulsion

Although it is more expensive than standard emulsion, this paint offers better coverage. It dries to give a similar sheen to kitchen/bathroom emulsion. If you are planning to apply a very light colour over a dark one, though, you may still need two coats.

Eggshell

An oil-based paint that offers a similar, but much more durable finish than that of vinyl silk, this is an ideal choice for woodwork. Some eggshell finishes are suitable for use on both walls and woodwork: use one of these when you want the two elements to match perfectly.

Satin finish

Similar to eggshell, this paint is easier to use and faster-drying.

Gloss

Usually oil-based, this is the most durable finish of all, but many people find its high shine too hard, unsubtle and unforgiving of even the smallest imperfections. Liquid gloss gives the smoothest finish, but the non-drip version is much easier to use.

Primer

This paint is used to seal bare, porous surfaces, such as plaster, wood or metal, and it comes in either water- or solvent-based versions.

To supplement their basic ranges, some manufacturers also produce a limited collection of novelty and faux finishes that are worth investigating. Among the most interesting of these are the mock-textile paints, which look astonishingly like corduroy, suede, taffeta or denim, and those that add a touch of funky (or retro) glamour in the form of pearly, sparkly or metallic finishes. Think, too, about how you might use some of the more mundane products such as blackboard paint or the updated, much subtler versions of old-fashioned textured paint in fresh, new ways.

historical paints

In addition to standard consumer paints, traditional alternatives are becoming increasingly widely available from specialist suppliers. Some of them require painstaking surface preparation and considerable practice and skill to apply effectively, but they all offer a combination of environmental friendliness and visual appeal that makes them well worth the effort. Also – unlike modern emulsions – most of these paints are very porous and so they can be used on new plaster. The most popular examples are:

Distemper (whitewash)

A mixture consisting of chalk, glue, natural pigment and water, distemper is associated with earthy, exotic shades of ochre and pale terracotta and deep, exotic ones such as ultramarine and viridian as well as pale ones. One of the most user-friendly of all the traditional finishes, distemper has a totally non-reflective surface with a velvety texture and an unparalleled intensity of colour. The characteristic powdery finish of traditional or 'soft' distemper, however, it tends to rub off, too, and is not washable.

Oil or casein-bound distemper

This paint, made with a base of oil or casein, a milk protein, is far more hard-wearing than its water-based equivalent.

An added advantage is that its classic matt finish can be wiped down.

Limewash

Although essentially matt in finish, this paint has a slightly light-reflective and mottled look. It is water resistant, with naturally antiseptic and insect-repelling qualities, but its major drawback is the caustic nature of its main ingredient.

1 When you set off in search of a particular shade of paint, take along an accurate colour reference: do not depend on vague descriptions, such as 'eau de nil' or 'Tuscan pink'.

2 Always buy enough paint to finish one room completely, since there is likely to be a colour variation between batches, even with stock colours. When your colour is specially mixed (or you are mixing it yourself), it's even more vital that you have enough paint to start with, since it's impossible to reproduce mixed colours exactly.

3 Keep any leftover paint so you can touch up accidental knocks. Instead of leaving it in a bulky tin, decant it into a glass jar, which takes up less space and allows instant identification.

4 In some cases, the right primer or undercoat is vital, so be sure to read the instructions on the tin. If disaster strikes, a helpline number is usually printed there as well.

5 Unless you're using a one-coat emulsion, plan on applying two coats of your chosen finish.

6 Never buy cheap paint. It is difficult to apply, it covers less well and you'll use more.

7 On the same principle, don't compromise on your equipment. A cheap paintbrush that sheds its bristles would be disastrous.

8 Stop painting at dusk. If you depend on artificial illumination, you'll wake up to a patchy finish.

organic paints

While most commercial paints, stains and varnishes are made from toxic petrochemicals, their organic equivalents contain only natural materials that are renewable, energy-efficient, bio-degradable, harmless to the ozone layer and not tested on animals. These natural ranges are now taking over an increasing proportion of the home-decorating market and they also include related products, such as adhesives and cleaning solutions.

Organic products offer three main advantages:

- They provide a much healthier atmosphere for those who have to live with them as well as those who apply them.
- They allow walls to 'breathe' properly, which offers protection for the fabric of any building.
- They are much more environmentally friendly.

paint effects

Towards the end of the twentieth century, the fashion for decorative paint effects completely dominated the fields of both interior design and DIY. Sadly, techniques that once seemed original and appealing became so overworked, fussy and ubiquitous (and, all too often, badly done) that they eventually fell out of favour. No-one would welcome the reappearance of these excesses in twenty-first century homes but, at the same time, it would be a great shame to dismiss them altogether. There are a considerable number of effects that, for surprisingly little cost and effort, offer subtle and achievable results that, in most cases, more closely resemble intriguing textures than small, busy patterns.

Originally, most paint effects were achieved by applying two layers of colour: an oil-based glaze on top of a matt ground. The pattern was created either by applying the glaze with a specialist tool, such as a brush, rag or natural sponge, according to the desired finish (the results are known as 'applied' finishes), or by covering the base with the glaze, then removing part of it in a similar way (known as 'subtracted' finishes). Oil-based glazes, although tricky to use and not environmentally friendly, were popular with the first wave of enthusiasts because they take ages to dry, so if a first attempt ended up in disaster, novice decorators could fiddle about with it as much as they liked until they got it right.

Since this factor really only comes into play with the intricate paint effects that defined the earlier fashion frenzy, most people now use modern water-based paints for both layers, thinning the top one with water if necessary, and this is a much easier process. To get the soft, all-over, broken-colour look that flatters so many rooms and wall surfaces, work with shades that are close to one another.

Colourwashing

One of the simplest and most appealing of all the paint effects, colourwashing produces the soft, irregular look of traditional distemper. In its subtle, modern incarnation, it involves applying a thinned layer of emulsion over a base coat of a very similar shade using a big, soft brush.

Sponging

Another easy technique, sponging involves using a natural marine sponge to apply (or subtract) the top layer of colour from the one underneath. As well as trying a variety of colours, you may also like to experiment with different kinds of sponge surfaces (big or little holes) and varying degrees of pressure.

Ragging

Achieved in the same way as sponging, ragging involves using a scrunched-up piece of cloth (or a plastic bag) instead of a sponge to apply (or subtract) the top layer of paint. The finished effect varies considerably depending on the material you choose.

Stippling & dragging

Both these techniques involve the use of a different, specialist brush. Stippling has a grainy, speckled look, while dragging produces subtle, uneven stripes. They are both difficult to master, easy to mess up and can even appear faintly passé in all but the most expert hands.

Faux finishes

Techniques originally used to imitate rarer or more costly surfaces are sometimes called 'faux' finishes. While these include such exotic effects as tortoiseshelling, bambooing and lacquering, the best known are probably marbling, crackle glazing and wood graining. On the whole, faux finishes are more suitable for decorating small pieces of furniture, accessories (like trays, boxes and curtain poles) and architectural details such as door frames and skirting boards, than as an all-over treatment for walls and ceilings. While creating very specialized finishes from scratch requires considerable skill and practice, the most popular are available in the form of easy-to-use DIY kits.

Stencilling & stamping

Like paint effects, stencilling has, in the past, been overdone. To make use of it in a fresh, new way, forget floral arrangements and conventional borders and build up your own witty effects, either by using existing stencils or cutting your own. Experiment with spray paint and proprietary crayons as well as standard liquid colours.

Decorative stamps, which give a similar look, are more limited in scope, but easier to use: either pick up the colour from an ink pad or apply it with a small roller. If you can't find any stamps you like, look for a specialist book that explains how to make your own from sheet rubber and wood or MDF offcuts.

FURTHER REFERENCE

The section highlights and describes the finishes that are most likely to suit your personal style and the rooms in your home, and it gives a brief idea of how difficult the main examples are to achieve. If you decide to try one of them, however, you should invest in a specialist book or leaflet that contains detailed, step-by-step instructions and a comprehensive list of required equipment and supplies. Or try one of the many videos, CD Roms, DVDs or courses now widely available.

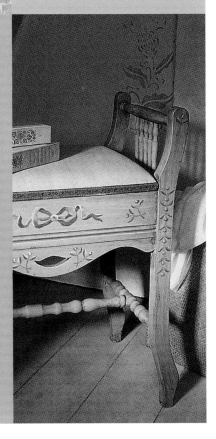

wallpaper

Papering your walls will never be as quick and easy as painting them, but if you love pattern, there is no more expansive surface on which to display it. The most conventional image of wallpaper is a historical one, and certainly, those with a weakness for Victorian or early twentieth-century rooms often find that hanging an appropriate paper is one of the most effective of all visual tricks for setting a historical scene.

Modern wallpaper ranges, however, include far more than museum-like reproductions and old-fashioned stripes and florals. If this is a decorating area that you haven't yet explored, you'll be surprised to find fresh, bright graphic shapes, primitive geometrics in warm, earthy tones, subtle surfaces that resemble skilful paint effects or natural

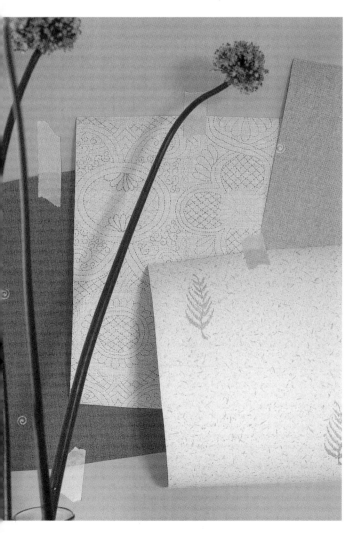

materials, like grass, raffia or bamboo, and paper-backed fabrics, such as silk, suede, leather, linen, hessian and felt. In parallel with the paint industry, wallpaper manufacturers have recently developed papers with light-reflecting pearlized, metallic and glittery finishes. For considerable extra cost, some can even be printed with your own drawings or photographs. Many of the most striking contemporary wallpapers, of course, aren't patterned at all in the conventional sense; instead, they provide large areas of pure, solid colour in a richly textured form.

Apart from looking out for the latest colours and finishes, another way to explore individual effects with wallpaper is to use it on one wall only. If you really aren't happy with the result, you won't have blown your budget and you can quickly strip it off again. Or, cut out one big block (or a collection of smaller shapes) from a dramatic design or colour and paste it onto the wall like a huge painting.

GLOSSARY

- **Embossed, textured, expanded** and **blown**, when applied to wallpaper, all indicate a raised pattern or texture intended to add visual interest or to conceal small cracks and bumps, or both.
- **Flocked wallpaper** also has a raised design, usually large, dark and swirly, picked out in cut-velvet pile. As a general rule, flocked papers are today found only in very old-fashioned restaurants and cool, ironic, post-modern decorating schemes.
- **Vinyl wallpaper** has a coating of PVC, which makes it durable and water resistant, and therefore particularly suitable for use in children's rooms, kitchens, bathrooms and other areas subjected to heavy wear. This protective surface has a very slight sheen.
- **Pre-pasted wallpaper** is supplied with a dry, adhesive backing and must be soaked in plain water, length by length, before it is hung. Special wallpaper troughs are available from decorating or DIY outlets.
- **Lining paper** is used underneath a decorative wallpaper to give it an even, professional finish when the underlying surface is uneven or covered with oil-based paint. When you want plain, smooth walls without having to replaster, hang thick lining paper that can be painted to give exactly the same effect.

1 Avoid cheap wallpapers since they're generally much more difficult to hang. Being thinner, they tend to tear and bubble more easily.

2 If you've never put up wallpaper before (or if you're papering a ceiling), ask an experienced friend or relative to help you, or find a dependable DIY manual, video, CD Rom or DVD that gives you all the information and advice you need.

3 As with paint, it's vital that all the rolls you use for one room carry the same batch number to avoid colour variations.

4 Big, regular patterns are much trickier to deal with than small, random ones because you have to match them from roll to roll. This also creates waste, so you have to buy more rolls.

5 You may already have most of the smaller items, such as scissors, a tape measure, bucket, sponge, etc., that you need for wallpapering. Wallpapering brushes can be borrowed or you can buy them fairly reasonably, and larger items, like a step ladder and pasting table, can be hired by the day.

Left: Flowery wallpaper needn't look boring and old-fashioned. Reinterpreted in zingy, modern colours and teamed with stylish furniture and accessories, it can considerably expand your decorating vocabulary.

fabric-covered
walls

Adorning walls with fabric in one form or another is one of the oldest of all decorative devices; in fact, wallpaper was originally invented as an affordable alternative to rich textiles and hangings. Infinitely flexible in terms of materials used and methods employed, fabric-covered walls can represent anything from a cheap and imaginative disguise for surfaces too horrible to contemplate, to the ultimate in interior luxury and extravagance. As well as its unique capacity for camouflage, fabric used in this way adds great warmth and style to a room and has the potential to improve both heat and sound insulation significantly. If you choose a suitable fixing method, you can even take it with you when you move and recycle it as cushions or curtains in your next home.

Depending on the overall look you're after, you can either stretch your fabric taut across the surface of the walls, or gather it in soft folds or tight ruching. The first option gives a neat, conventional, wallpaper-like effect, but it can also be slightly fiddly to do since – unless your room is very small and your fabric very wide – you will have to seam two or more widths of material together before attaching it flush to the wall. Although there are several systems on the market designed to fasten the resulting panels in position (usually with teeth or clips set into lengths of track), one of the simplest and cheapest devices involves fixing thin wooden battens to the top and bottom of the wall, then stapling the fabric onto (or wrapping it around) them. Disguise the staples with lengths of plain tape, braid or perhaps ribbon or velvet trim. Or, to allow

TOP TIPS

1 Avoid using fabric on damp walls or those where condensation is a problem since mildew is likely to set in.
2 Strong food smells cling to fabrics so this is not a suitable treatment for dining rooms.
3 An all-over spray with proprietary stain protector will keep dust and grime at bay.
4 Any material that stretches easily is best suited to gentle gathers since attempting to pull it flat may result in sagging.

MATERIAL WORLDS

Whatever impression you wish to create, there are plenty of inexpensive fabrics that will do the job. If you're willing to sacrifice practicality for exotic allure (in a short-term rental, for example), your choice will be even wider. Look out for the following materials:

- muslin or mosquito netting (for walls and ceilings)
- cotton sheeting
- calico
- ticking
- canvas or duck
- exhibition felt
- curtain lining
- anything sequined or glittery from a theatrical supplier

Opposite: Fabric-lined walls offer a depth of colour and visual warmth that paper can't match. Here, simple checked cotton establishes the room's decorative theme.

This page: Create giant stripes with floor-to-ceiling banners spaced out along a plain wall. Note the painted table, which echoes the two-tone motif.

the fabric to be removed for washing later on, attach it with Velcro instead. For a subtle, padded look and to provide an extra layer of insulation, line the walls initially with a thick sheet of synthetic wadding.

Unlike large flat panels, gathered fabric can give several very different looks according to the type of gathers you choose. Tight ruching is comparatively regular and formal (and also requires a great deal of material). Fix it in the same way as fabric panels by using a track system, or staple it directly onto wooden battens. The looser and more uneven the folds, the softer the final effect will be. For a very adaptable and appealing look, gather your fabric from the top only, or don't gather it at all: just stitch a row of small curtain rings along the top of the fabric and loop them over matching, wall-fixed hooks. If your walls are divided into sections with elegant moulding, try hanging gently gathered 'curtains' from the picture rail to the floor, or between the picture and the dado rails, instead of covering the whole surface.

panelling

In a similar way to hanging fabric on walls, covering them with timber panelling is a treatment that not only looks timeless and classy, it also has the potential to solve a mixed bag of decorating problems at a stroke. In all its forms, wall panelling provides the highest level of heat and sound insulation of any standard covering. It conceals not only disfigured surfaces, but also clumsy and dust-collecting runs of pipework; it is so durable, and its surface is so tough that it never needs replacing, and it can lend itself to almost any decorating style.

The most elaborate and costly panels of all are richly carved from precious hardwood into traditional linenfold shapes or embellished with garlands of fruit or classical detailing. Most of us only ever see examples such as these in museums and historic houses, but architectural salvage companies sometimes rescue pieces from building sites and offer them for sale. If the period look is what you're after, good reproductions may be the answer. Unfortunately, reproduction panelling – like the real thing – is not for paupers, but there is a cut-price option: sheets of ready-to-paint MDF (medium-density fibreboard) that have been carefully shaped and detailed to resemble carved timber.

The cheapest, the most versatile (in both practical and aesthetic terms) and one of the more stylish panelling options is the ordinary tongue-and-groove cladding that we traditionally associate with rustic cottages, American colonial houses and Swedish country style (see page 33). Usually made from pine, it is available in several different widths and is just as suitable for use on ceilings and doors as walls. If the necessity for camouflage is overwhelming, fix the cladding to run vertically from cornice (or picture rail) to skirting. Alternatively, put up a useful shelf or peg rail to run all around the room at shoulder height and then clad just the area below it. You can also protect the particularly vulnerable section of wall beneath the dado rail in the same way.

In the living room, bedroom, kitchen or entrance hall, use tongue-and-groove cladding to build rows of fitted storage cupboards that blend seamlessly into the woodwork. Install your cladding horizontally to dado height in the bathroom. As well as boxing-in ugly pipes here, it will also cover your bath panel, protect the walls from the inevitable splashes of water and – as an added bonus – increase the impression of space in this, the smallest of rooms.

Opposite: The simple painted cladding in this French country retreat was deliberately installed in the form of rough planks instead of the more conventional tongue-and-groove boards. To accentuate the rustic effect overall, the spacing between them was varied almost imperceptibly.

TOP TIPS

1 Make sure all traces of damp have been treated before timber panelling is fixed to any wall. If in doubt, seek professional advice.

2 If you're planning to create striped walls with tongue-and-groove cladding (for a fresh fairground or seaside scheme, perhaps), ensure perfect edges by painting each board separately before you slot them all together.

3 Fixing tongue-and-groove boards is well within the ability of amateur carpenters or DIY enthusiasts. Those who are completely inexperienced, however, may find the technique requires a bit of practice. Putting up intricate old or reproduction panelling, on the other hand, is most definitely an expert's job.

4 Timber panelling with a natural waxed finish should be dusted regularly with a damp cloth and polished gently every few months.

5 The ultimate in low-cost laziness (but a surprisingly effective technique) is to create your own tongue-and-groove cladding by cutting grooves into a large sheet of MDF spaced at regular intervals before you fix it in position.

FLOORS

A stylish floor covering will lift your rooms instantly and enhance their impression of comfort. In the same way, ugly, stained or worn floors create an air of decay and grubbiness that won't go away until they do. The fact that more of your budget is likely to be taken up by floor coverings than any other element is due partly to the fact that after walls, floors cover the largest area in your home. Unlike walls, though, they have to withstand constant wear and damaging grime, either tracked in from outside or deposited by gravity.

Despite this tight brief, however, finding an appropriate floor covering simply involves identifying a combination of style and practicality that works for you. Floor covering trends seem to change more often – and more violently – than those in other design areas, however, so it's easy for the novice to feel intimidated, but try to keep your head: the only thing more foolish than choosing an unsuitable floor on the basis of its street cred is rejecting one that meets all your needs just because it was last year's hot news.

flooring types

Floor coverings are grouped under four basic headings:

- **Soft flooring** (carpets, rugs and natural coverings like coir and sisal)
- **Wood flooring** (including bamboo and man-made boards)
- **Resilient flooring** (vinyl, linoleum, rubber, cork and leather)
- **Hard flooring** (stone, concrete, metal and tiles – ceramic, quarry, etc.)

When it comes to choosing between these surfaces, it's easy to be swayed by appearance alone, but there are a number of other factors to keep in mind:

- **Durability** How much wear will the floor get? (Some are tougher than others.)
- **Noise level** The harder the surface, the noisier it is, and downstairs neighbours will suffer more than those next door.
- **Access** Do any major pipes, wires or ducts run underneath the floor? If so, make sure you still have access to them once the floor has been laid.
- **Temperature** Soft flooring is the most efficient insulator of all, whereas old floorboards can let through howling draughts.
- **Absorbency** Many floor coverings are vulnerable to damp, so they are unsuitable for rooms where water gets splashed about.
- **Hygiene** Choose washable floors for bathrooms and kitchens.
- **Installation** Some flooring requires special underlay and skilled fitting. If you can't afford the whole package, either wait or choose something else instead.

Whatever flooring you choose, it will need an even, stable base, which means sorting out bumpy boards. Sometimes this may involve laying a subfloor. If you ignore this requirement, your covering will look lumpy and wear far more quickly.

TOP TIPS

1 Make a rough drawing of each room, noting its dimensions and the position and size of any projections or irregularities. Later on, when you're considering several floor-covering options in different widths or lengths, this information may have a huge bearing on how much you need and therefore on the final cost.
2 Try to get hold of a large sample of your chosen flooring so that you can see it lying flat, in situ and under different lighting conditions. Most flooring looks very different viewed from a distance, covering a large surface, so if you can't see the one you like in a room set, ask if there are any promotional photographs available.
3 Protect your floors by fitting every item of heavy furniture (bed, sofa, etc.) with castors.
4 When you arrange to have flooring installed, make sure you are fully aware of any relevant tasks you are responsible for, such as taking up existing carpet or clearing furniture out of the room.

Opposite: In the sunny stairwell of this sleek loft conversion, pale, wide floorboards alternate with strips of toughened glass to allow light to filter through to the living space below. Note the wire balustrade whose graphic grid construction reinforces the industrial theme of the apartment.

soft flooring

When you want an atmosphere of warmth and comfort, it's hard to beat fitted soft flooring: either carpet or a 'natural' alternative like coir or jute. Combined with thick underlay, it muffles sound, keeps in warmth, minimizes draughts and provides a tactile surface underfoot. This option is best avoided, though, where damp is a problem, in food preparation areas or anywhere vulnerable to water. Some types harbour animal hairs and dust, too, which may affect allergy sufferers. Soft flooring comes in a vast range of designs, weaves, colours and fibres to suit every taste, location and budget. Plain colours create a more spacious impression than patterns and they are easier to coordinate with other furnishings, but there are a great many stylish patterned carpets around, so if one of them captures your imagination, go for it. The premise, however, that patterns are best because they camouflage dirt is not only flawed, it is also faintly unsavoury. Try, however, to stay away from very pale colours and very dark ones, both of which show every mark.

CARPET TYPES

The quality of a carpet is determined by its construction, the nature of its pile and the material it is made from. Woven carpets – the very best – are produced on looms that weave backing and pile simultaneously. These are referred to as 'Wilton' or 'Axminster', according to the weaving method used. Wilton looms tend to produce plain carpets, while Axminster looms are used to create patterns. Most domestic carpets, however, are made by a less costly method in which the yarn is stitched into a pre-woven backing; these are known as 'tufted carpets'. There are four main types: loop pile, velvet pile, twist pile and shag pile (see opposite). When the pile is cut into different heights and/or combined with loop pile to form figured designs, it is called sculptured pile. At the bottom end of the market are bonded carpets, in which the pile is stuck onto the backing instead of stitched into it, as with tufted carpets.

When it comes to content, wool is the fibre of choice: it looks and feels wonderful, it's tough, fire resistant, anti-static, natural and expensive. While synthetic fibres cost less and wear well, they are no competition for the real thing. A blend (about 80:20) of wool with a man-made material like nylon is an affordable compromise.

GRADES OF CARPET

Every carpet is graded according to durability. Grading varies, but differentiates between carpets intended for areas of heavy wear and those suitable only for light traffic. Quality carpets are hessian-backed, need separate underlay and should be professionally fitted. Foam-backed carpets tend to be less expensive (and require neither underlay nor skilled fitting), but are less likely to offer long-term value for money. To keep costs down without compromising on quality, look for premium lines that have been reduced because the range is discontinued or there is a flaw in the pile. Or check to see if an unlucky combination of room size and roll width results in excess waste; you may need less of a similar carpet in a different width.

TUFTED CARPETS

Loop pile carpets are so-called because the loops that are formed when the yarn is stitched into the backing are left uncut to give the surface its knobbly texture (left and far left).

Velvet (or velours) pile has been cut, then closely sheared to produce a smooth, luxurious finish. Like the fabric it's named after, velvet pile is prone to shading.

Twist pile has been cut and tightly twisted, then heat set to make it especially durable as well as less prone to shading, tracking and shedding fluff.

Shag pile is cut much longer than velvet or twist pile to give a soft, deep look and feel. A similar, but slightly shorter pile than shag pile is known as **Saxony**.

natural floor coverings

In this context, the term 'natural' generally refers to a particular style of flatweave matting, carpet or rug (i.e. one with no pile) that has been woven from a plant fibre such as sisal, coir, jute, seagrass or rush. In common use all over the world for centuries, these materials still work well in almost any room and complement a wide range of design styles.

In their most recognizable form, natural floor coverings come in an appealing palette of warm natural colours, although dyed versions is also available on the market. Textures, too, vary widely according to the type of fibre involved. Usually backed with latex, natural flooring tends to be woven in either traditional cord, chevron or basketweave patterns, and it is sold on wide rolls (and sometimes as bound area rugs) in exactly the same way as conventional carpet.

Environmentally friendly and totally renewable, these fibres are anti-static and they don't harbour dust, which makes them a particularly suitable choice if you are prone to allergies. They are also easy to vacuum, but tend to stain easily and permanently, and most cannot be washed with soap and water. Some types are relatively cheap, while others are extremely expensive, but all of them should be laid by a professional fitter.

- **Sisal** is smooth and slightly shiny, with a slightly scratchy feel, and a naturally golden colour. Tough and practical, it is one of the most expensive of all the options for flooring fibres.
- **Coir** (above left), is made from coconut husks, is much cheaper than sisal, but equally durable. It has a distinctively rough, coarse surface.
- **Jute** has a comparatively soft feel, but is less hardwearing than most other materials in the same family of fibres.
- **Seagrass** has a faintly greenish tinge and a tough, smooth and almost waxy surface, so it won't stain as readily as some natural fibres. It dries out quickly, though, and snags easily.
- **Rush** can take the form of inexpensive loose mats or very costly ones with a strong medieval look, which are assembled from handwoven and plaited strips. These strips can also be used to make a fully fitted floor covering. Like seagrass, rush needs to be kept slightly damp, so if you can afford a suitable quality, consider this floor covering option for use in either a basement or perhaps a conservatory.
- **Paper** (left) the newest natural flooring material on the market, has long been in use in the Far East. It has cleaner lines and a more sharply defined weave than any other fibre, and its twisted construction and waxy finish make it very strong. Paper floors are unsuitable in any areas that are subject to damp.
- **Flatweave** wool offers the best of all worlds in many ways since it combines the subtle, natural colours and weaves typical of coir and sisal with the softness, durability and easy-care qualities of wool.

rugs

There are few furnishing elements that can equal rugs when it comes to delivering a wide range of decorative effects for very little money. Available in an astounding variety of sizes, colours, patterns and fibres, they can inject fresh colour and texture into an otherwise boring scheme, hide stains or bald and fraying patches on an old carpet and prevent similar damage to a new one. They can be used to decorate walls, too. Look for woven cotton, traditional kelims, shaggy or fluffy rugs in funky colours, or even plain white for girly glamour (left), or experiment with classic squares cut from natural flooring and bound with tape. If you have a creative streak, try painting your own canvas floorcloths with fabric paint and pre-cut stencils or create your own designs freehand.

TOP TIPS

1 Even if the label states 'dryclean only', most small cotton rugs will go in your washing machine on a cool cycle. As many of these cost less than a few trips to the drycleaners, you can't really lose. The dyes are unlikely to be stable, though, so wash rugs separately.

2 When you place a coloured rug on a pale carpet make sure the dye won't bleed through. If in doubt, slip a barrier (a sheet of plastic, perhaps) between them, or choose an undyed rug instead.

3 Loose rugs should never be placed directly on a hard floor. To guard against accidents, anchor them with an anti-slip mat or special tape.

Smooth blond hardwood laid in the
form of narrow boards establishes
the clean, light and very natural style
of this airy loft bedroom.

wood flooring

Beautiful, easy to maintain and infinitely adaptable, wood flooring provides a unique blend of sleek, uncluttered lines and warm, natural tones that ensure it never goes out of fashion. Less yielding underfoot than carpet, it offers a more inviting surface than stone or ceramic tiles. In all its forms, however, it tends to be noisy, vulnerable to moisture in any significant degree and slippery when wet.

The most expensive, and the most durable, wood flooring is made from hard timbers such as oak, birch, maple or one of the tropical hardwoods (iroko, sapele, etc.), while at the cheaper end of the market, softwood of some kind (usually pine but sometimes spruce) is the main choice. However, softwood is much more vulnerable to scratches, dents, warping and general wear and tear.

There are three main kinds of timber flooring: solid, veneered and laminate:

- **Solid timber flooring** is available as conventional planks or boards (unfinished or pre-sealed) in a variety of widths; as strip flooring (pre-sealed sections that slot together); block flooring (small squares that are individually glued to a subfloor to make a pattern) or parquet, sometimes known as mosaic block flooring (panels of pre-assembled hardwood strips). Solid wood floors are costly, but they can be endlessly sanded and re-finished, and they not only last indefinitely, but often improve with age as well.
- **Veneered flooring** consists of a top layer of hardwood or softwood that is bonded to a base material. Available as planks and blocks, it comes in a wide range of prices depending on the thickness of the veneer and the timber used. Many examples are considerably cheaper than solid floors, while others cost almost as much, but none are as durable.
- **Laminate flooring** is the cheapest of the three options. Because its surface is actually a photograph of woodgrain printed onto a softwood base, then coated with tough vinyl or PVC, it is very easy to look after and extremely hard-wearing. Once damaged, of course, it cannot be sanded or re-finished.

Another economical flooring option is plain hardboard or plywood. Available in large sheets or square tiles, it has a pale, smooth, regular surface that's ready for painting, staining or varnishing. MDF can be used in the same way, but its extreme porosity makes it more troublesome to finish.

If you discover old boards under the existing flooring and they're in good condition, consider having them stripped. You can, of course, do this yourself with a hired sander, but it's a filthy, time-consuming, back-breaking job, so don't take it on lightly. Once the sanding is done, your floor is ready to be finished. Choose wax, oil or varnish (matt or satin rather than gloss) and apply it to the bare wood for a subtle, natural look. If you want a darker or lighter tone, bleach or stain the timber before you add your chosen finish. Alternatively, create a more decorative look with floor paint, dye or colourwash.

TOP TIPS

1 Solid timber flooring should always be fitted by an expert. Laminates and veneers that are suitable for DIY installation will be clearly labelled and come with full instructions.
2 Although wide planks usually have a higher unit cost than narrow ones or small blocks, they are simpler (and therefore cheaper) to lay.
3 Check out architectural salvage companies for reclaimed timber flooring, which offers instant character as well as environmental credibility.
4 To remove surface grime, wipe your floor with a damp cloth or mop rather than over-wetting it.

A fairly recent addition to the flooring market, bamboo (shown) is stronger and more stable than wood. It also has a higher resistance to moisture. Sold in laminated, tongue-and-groove planks (lacquered or unfinished), bamboo flooring represents the ultimate in eco-chic with its cool, pale allure and impeccable credentials as the ultimate renewable resource: bamboo is the fastest-growing plant in existence. In price, it compares well with solid wood.

resilient flooring

The materials that fall under this heading – linoleum, vinyl, cork, rubber and leather – cannot accurately be described as soft or hard. They are smoother, tougher and easier to maintain than carpet or nature-fibre flooring, yet most feel warmer, more springy to the touch than any hard floor, including wood. All resilient flooring is sold in tile form, and some types (lino and vinyl, for example) come in rolls as well. Tiles are much easier to lay than sheet flooring. Choose a solid block of one colour, or arrange contrasting tiles in a traditional chequerboard pattern. In terms of style and price, there is a resilient floor to suit everyone. A few vinyl and cork ranges are extremely cheap, while leather floors represent the very top end of the market. A word of caution: Some resilient flooring can be damaged irreparably if you use the wrong cleaning solution, so read the manufacturer's care instructions.

Linoleum

Invented in 1861, lino is enjoying a revival in popularity after years of neglect. A natural product made of cork, woodflour, linseed oil and resin, it is thick and warm to the touch with enough 'give' to make it comfortable to walk on. It's also hard-wearing, anti-static, anti-bacterial and resistant to burns and scratches. Lino will survive splashes or drips, but constant flooding causes serious damage, and sharp objects like stiletto heels will dent it. Available in plain colours and lots of patterns, from subtle speckles to intricate floral and geometric motifs, lino comes in both sheet and tile form. Both types can be cut and glued to form simple but effective designs. Although the discovery of the cheaper vinyl flooring in the 1960s helped to destroy its market domination, modern lino costs less than many ranges of vinyl.

Vinyl

The synthetic version of lino, vinyl is also available in sheet and tile form. These vary widely in terms of thickness, weight, flexibility, type of backing, surface coating and, of course, price. Vinyl, too, can be cut and re-assembled to create unique patterns, and most ranges include not only plain colours and subtle textures but also a number of designs that imitate materials such as marble, oak, metal and glass. Waterproof and easy to clean, vinyl is a popular choice for kitchen and bathroom floors. The more expensive cushion vinyls are softer underfoot than solid ones, and offer considerably more effective sound and heat insulation.

Cork

Another traditional flooring whose comeback is long overdue, cork is practical, warm, excellent for insulation and very easy to install. Iin the form of unsealed tiles, it is also one of the most affordable of all resilient floors. More sophisticated versions, however, involve bonding a cork veneer onto multi-layered tongue-and-groove planks, and are therefore much more costly. A natural product, cork is also a sound environmental choice. In its original state, it is either a golden honey colour or a deep brown, but most modern ranges include a few bright colours as well. Unsealed cork tiles require several coats of clear varnish or sealant. If you

Use vinyl or lino to create a unique fantasy floor, cutting out your pattern and piecing it together like a giant mosaic. To focus attention on an elaborate design, keep all the other elements in the room low key.

want to add a touch of colour, brush on a coat of an emulsion paint or a spirit-based wood stain first.

Rubber

Very popular with designers and architects, rubber flooring is sold in a fantastic array of exciting shades and special finishes, including marbled, 1950s-style flecked and terrazzo. Some manufacturers will even match any colour or pattern you specify. Available only in tiles of varying sizes, rubber flooring is undoubtedly an expensive option, but it has a singularly clean and contemporary look, it's tough, warm, nice to walk on and good for muffling noise. Completely waterproof, rubber is an excellent choice for kitchens and bathrooms, and comes in a huge variety of interesting textures that create a safe, non-slip surface. Unfortunately, these surfaces also have a tendency to trap dirt. They should be given occasional coat of proprietary polish, but from day to day, all they need is washing with mild detergent solution followed by a thorough rinse.

Leather

Like all leather surfaces, leather flooring (sold in tiles as well as irregularly shaped sheets) is incredibly durable, it looks fantastic and has an intoxicating smell. While leather is vulnerable to scuffs and scratches, regular waxing will blend them into a rich, characterful patina that deepens attractively with age. Leather flooring is not suitable for use in kitchens or bathrooms and it represents a very serious financial outlay indeed.

hard flooring

When it comes to flooring, the term 'hard' means exactly what it says: stone, tiles, brick, concrete and metal all fall into this category. Equally appropriate both inside and out, hard floors can last forever. They are completely waterproof, easy to clean and suitable for use with underfloor heating. On the down side, they feel cold and unyielding underfoot and they are very likely to damage any unfortunate object, or indeed person, that makes unexpected contact with them. Hard floors are also extremely heavy, which rules them out for most upstairs rooms. However, they are always a practical choice in entrance halls, bathrooms, kitchens and conservatories. In sultry tropical regions, their cool smoothness makes them a popular choice in every other room as well, but in chillier climes, most people prefer the warmth of carpet or wood in areas associated with rest and relaxation.

STONE

Most of the different types of stone flooring are sold either as large slabs (flagstones) or conventional tiles (left).

- **Limestone** is pale and grainy, with a textured surface that improves with age.
- **Granite** is extremely hard and has a speckly finish. It is usually grey or black, but pink, green and rusty red granites are not uncommon.
- **Slate** has a rippled texture and comes in a range of subtle, darkish hues.
- **Marble**, with its rich colouring and delicate veins, offers the ultimate in luxury at an appropriate price. Cold and slippery underfoot, it stains easily and should be polished often.
- **Terrazzo** is made from marble chippings mixed with concrete to produce tough, textured flooring in a variety of mottled colours.

FLOORING TILES

Ceramic, terracotta and quarry tiles and flooring bricks (known as 'pavers') are all made from clay that has been shaped and fired in a kiln. Glazed tiles are easy to maintain but their glossy surface is vulnerable to chips and scratches. Left unglazed, they have a more rustic, natural look and are less slippery (left).

- **Ceramic** tiles are produced in a wide range of prices, colours, shapes and patterns. Most of them are machine made, but a range of hand-painted and hand-moulded designs is also available.
- **Terracotta** tiles are sold in a limited palette of earth colours. They are fairly porous and tend to retain heat, which makes them warmer underfoot than many other types of tile.
- **Quarry** tiles have a similarly rustic appeal, but they are fired at a much higher temperature than terracotta, which makes them considerably tougher. Prices vary depending on thickness.
- **Brick pavers/flooring bricks** (especially old ones) have a strong, traditional charm of their own. Usually laid out in a rhythmic pattern (herringbone or basketweave, for example), they make a durable, non-slip floor surface that requires no special treatment.

1 Most hard flooring should be installed by a professional. Check with your retailer.

2 When a patio or terrace leads off the kitchen or conservatory, try laying the same surface throughout. It looks attractive and makes the space more 'pulled together'.

3 Some stone and ceramic flooring needs to be treated with a sealant and some doesn't. Since the different varieties of a particular material don't all necessarily require the same treatment, however, it's impossible to provide general guidelines. Check with your retailer.

4 Almost every hard floor can be painted. Make sure, though, that the paint you use is suitable for the surface involved.

CONCRETE

New concrete flooring can either be laid as pre-cast slabs or poured wet in situ, then smoothed out and left to dry. In both forms, it is remarkably cheap and virtually indestructible. It is brutally industrial in appearance, however, and as a general rule, more people are stuck with these floors than choose them. If you are faced with a bleak expanse of bare concrete, try humanizing it with colour in the form of a low-sheen floor paint or a translucent tint or stain. Alternatively, for a surprisingly rich, subtle finish, consider oiling or perhaps waxing the surface instead.

METAL

Another quintessentially industrial option, metal flooring (stainless steel or aluminium) comes in either tile or sheet form, both of which have a ridged, non-slip surface. Metal floors are expensive but incredibly hard-wearing and fairly easy to install for any skilled DIY enthusiast. Although a vacuum cleaner will get rid of dust and fluff, any grime that collects in the ridges can be shifted only by using elbow grease. Unless this is a prospect you particularly relish, avoid laying metal flooring over large areas.

Left: Subtly textured and gently waxed, this poured concrete floor manages to look natural and interesting rather than brutal and cold.

WINDOWS

Window treatments are chosen primarily to suit their surrounding design landscape, but their power and influence extends well beyond aesthetics. The most basic function of curtains or blinds is to afford privacy by protecting both rooms and their inhabitants from general scrutiny. Ensuring privacy, of course, also strengthens security because thieves are more likely to break in if they spot saleable goods.

Strong sunlight fades colours and weakens fibres, and so another important function of well-chosen window treatments is to shade the surfaces and objects inside. In a perfect world, all windows would frame an uplifting view of the outside world, but when reality lets us down and a little camouflage is called for, an artfully arranged drape or panel will usually do the trick.

Window coverings fall into three broad categories – curtains, blinds and shutters. However, these can be interpreted, as well as combined, in endless imaginative ways. You may decide to choose a different window treatment and material for each of your rooms, or to establish a strong decorative theme by dressing all your windows (except those in the bathroom and kitchen) identically. Alternatively, you could perhaps suggest a more subtle link by using exactly the same fabric throughout your home, but the style could be varied from room to room: long curtains in the living room, say, perhaps soft blinds in the bedroom and hinged fabric panels for small windows in the hall. Keep in mind, though, that within the same room, all the windows should match.

making your choice

When you're weighing up the options, take the following points into consideration:

Curtains

There's no doubt that panels of softly draped fabric have a softening effect on both windows and rooms, and they can help to create an atmosphere of warmth and cosiness. In some schemes (those with a formal, period look, for example), they are an important element. Curtains, especially long, thick ones, are excellent for keeping out cold, draughts and noise, and they offer enormous scope for camouflaging ill-proportioned or ugly windows. Gathered fabric tends to harbour dust, however, and this may rule it out for allergy sufferers. Although costs can vary wildly with all window treatments depending on the materials used and the size and complexity of their design, curtains tend to be the most expensive choice.

Blinds

Most varieties of blind have spare, graphic lines, which make them particularly suitable for modern rooms. Easy to clean, they take up less space than curtains, and many of the most popular types (roller and London, for example) are cheaper too. This is partly because less fabric is required for blinds, but also because they are simpler to make and hang. Again, though, the more exotic and sophisticated designs will always cost more than plain, basic curtains. Blinds provide little heat or sound insulation, and their capacity to alter the visual perception of a window's shape or size is limited, although it varies from one type of blind to another.

Shutters

Usually made of wood, shutters have a solid, pared-down look that suits many decorating styles. They can be used to block out the sun completely, and those fitted with bars and/or locks provide invaluable extra security. Hinged screens and flat panels in a variety of different materials have a similar feel to shutters.

Whatever window treatment (or treatments) you prefer, keep your choices simple. Elaborate swags, pelmets, ruffles, borders and painted motifs belong to an earlier, much fussier age. Instead, concentrate on interesting fabrics, good design and subtle detailing.

Opposite: Hinged panel shutters offer stylistic neutrality in a room that combines Neoclassical architecture and detailing with 1960s retro furnishings. The panels cover the glass at night to ensure the security of this vulnerable garden window, yet fold back completely to reveal the stunning view.

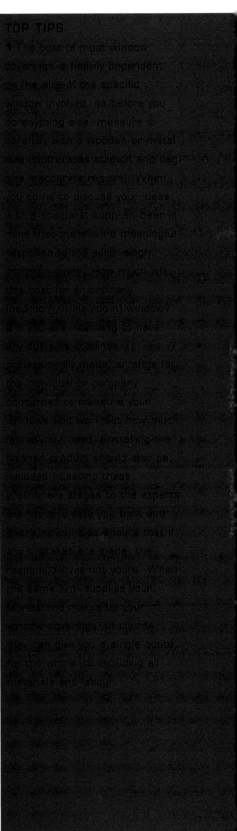

curtains

With their unique blend of decorative appeal and multi-faceted practicality, curtains still lead the field when it comes to dressing domestic windows. The most graceful and flattering styles tend to be full-length and hang so they are just touching the floor, or drooping over it in a soft pool of fabric. If you decide against long curtains, the only acceptable alternative is short ones that finish just below the window sill. Any length hovering between long and short, however, gives an unfortunate half-mast effect.

The next decision you face is whether to have your curtains lined or unlined. Lining helps them to hang better, it protects the fabric from dirt and strong sunlight (both of which cause fading and rot), and it dims early morning rays that might wake you prematurely. Lining all your curtains to match also gives a neat, coordinated look from the outside. As well as basic linings, look for those that block out the light completely, add a flame-retardant layer or provide extra insulation. Interlining, a layer of padding between curtain and lining, gives an opulent, formal appearance and increases both thermal and sound insulation significantly. Similarly, if an ill-fitting front door lets in cold air, hang an interlined curtain in front of it, which you can then pull across when you've settled in for the night.

Unlined curtains have a natural, artless charm of their own that should not be spoilt by elaborate headings or overly fussy trims. Whether they are short and crisp, or long and floaty, they have the potential to filter the light in prettily, especially when the weave has been chosen with this in mind: hand-loomed cotton, slubby linen or watery silk, perhaps. Net curtains, also known as sheers, are light and translucent. Designed to cover the glass permanently under conventional curtains, they allow you to see out of your rooms during the day while protecting your privacy by preventing any passers-by from looking in.

POLES, RODS & TRACKS

Most curtains are suspended by a row of hooks from some kind of pole, rod or track. Styles vary according to the weight of the curtains and the shape of the window, as well as personal preference. For most rooms and most styles of curtain, though, simple poles slotted into sturdy brackets

offer a practical as well as an elegant means of support. Buy purpose-designed poles made of wood, brass, chrome, cast iron or perspex, or you could even improvise your own. Try copper, brass or steel tubing, towel rails, garden cane or wooden dowelling to hold lightweight curtains, such as muslins and sheers and thick broom handles or even a pair of sturdy oars to cope with the longer, heavier ones like velvets and brocades.

In terms of track, slim and flexible aluminium designs have a certain functional honesty and they are the only feasible option when you're faced with all the angles and curves associated with traditional bay and bow windows. Flimsy, plastic versions of track were a popular choice in the days when pelmets and valances were on hand to hide them from view, but they are singularly unappealing and unsuitable for display. Some tracks come complete with a clever corded pulley system that allows you to open and close your curtains without touching them. This is a worthwhile consideration for pale, easily soiled fabrics, or those with an obvious pile that constant handling over time may damage.

HEADINGS & TIE-BACKS

The way your curtains hang is governed by the style of heading you choose. Most traditional curtain headings are created by drawing up a pair of cords which are threaded through a band of heading tape sewn onto the back of each curtain. Different tapes form different styles of heading (see page 87). Headings with separate pleats or folds can also be stitched by hand without using heading tape, but this is an exacting and expensive process, and best avoided by the complete beginner. Another popular – and very simple – alternative is to gather the curtains directly onto a pole. To do this, either pass the pole through a row of tabs, ties or eyelets, or slot it through a wide hem or casing.

Another traditional convention that – like the curtain pole – is fun to interpret in fresh ways is that of tying curtains neatly back at each side to form a set of graceful drapes and admit more light into the room at the same time. This is done by tucking them behind large knobs or metal hooks screwed into the wall, or by catching them in corded tassels or special tie-backs made from matching fabric. All these devices work well and the commercial versions have widened their appeal considerably in recent years. Look for sleek hooks in chrome, brass and cast iron, and tassels made from natural cotton and jute. Or create your own tie-backs with leather belts, lengths of rope, chain or rubber webbing, or anything else that sparks your imagination.

Left: Long, filmy curtains frame a glazed garden door prettily, and blow gently in the summer breeze to reinforce the link between inside and out. Note the subtle floral motif woven into the fabric.

TOP TIPS

1 It's now easier than ever before to buy smart and affordable ready-made curtains. Neatly filling the wide price gap between bespoke and homemade versions, off-the-peg curtains come in many different sizes, fabrics and headings.

2 Cleverly arranged curtains can alter the apparent shape or position of your windows. To disguise a narrow window, extend the track or pole well beyond the frame on either side. If you want to make a window appear taller, fix the track at an appropriate distance above the frame, then bridge the gap with a plain pelmet or valance. When you're faced with several windows (identical or odd) side by side, give the room a sense of visual cohesion by hanging an uninterrupted expanse of curtain across the entire wall.

3 To hang a curtain at a deeply recessed window without blocking the light with its fullness, look for a single, hinged rod that swings out from one side like a towel rail.

4 Ensure maximum privacy while admitting as much available light as possible by hanging a set of traditional café curtains from a slim rod fixed across the middle of the window.

1 If you're making your own curtains, measure the relevant width of the pole or track (rather than the window) and the 'drop' (the distance from wherever the hooks will hang – the bottom of the track or the rings – to the hem). Choose your heading and then seek expert guidance to work out exactly how much fabric you'll need.

2 When you draw up the heading-tape cords on new curtains, there will be a considerable excess at one end. Don't cut this off; instead, tie it in a loose bow or wind it around a large safety pin so you can pull the curtains flat again for cleaning (or re-adjust their fullness for use elsewhere).

3 Fixing a radiator directly beneath a window not only makes long curtains impractical, it also results in a considerable waste of heat. If at all possible, have the radiator moved to another part of the room. Or create a decorative illusion by fixing a plain blind to do all the work and hanging dress (false) curtains on either side.

Left: Thick golden tassels anchor one of the heavy scarlet curtains that make a perfect frame for this tall period window. Covering the glass is a sheer monogrammed panel decorated with subtle drawn-thread work.

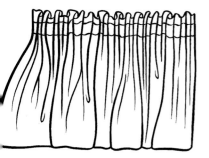

Gathered heading

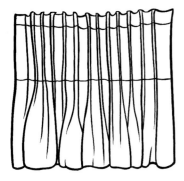

Pencil pleats

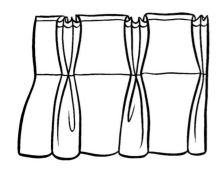

Pinch pleats

Box pleats

CURTAIN HEADINGS

The most popular styles of curtain heading are:

- **Gathered or standard headings** draw fabric into irregular folds, which particularly suit lightweight, unlined styles and short, informal treatments.
- **Pencil pleats** are simple, elegant, and appropriate for any fabric or style. They require fabric fullness of at least twice the width of the pole or track.
- **Pinch pleats** create a formal, traditional effect. Regular and deep, they also need twice the width of the pole in fullness.
- **Box pleats** are even more controlled than pinch pleats and they produce a similar look. Two-and-a-half times the width of the pole in fullness is required.
- **Cartridge pleats** resemble plump, widely spaced pencil pleats. To emphasize their rounded shape, they are sometimes filled with wadding. Two-and-a-half times the width of the pole is the required fullness.
- **Tabs or ties** can either be made to match the curtains, known as self-tabs or ties, or improvised with ribbon, braid or twine, or even shoe laces.
- **Eyelets**, if they're large enough, can slot directly over a slim curtain rod. Otherwise, thread a tie through each eyelet (or one continuous tie through them all).
- **Cased headings** involve gathering the curtains directly onto a pole through a deep hem, or a length of wide tape stitched onto the back. Alternatively, thread the pole through a wide decorative ribbon sewn onto the front.

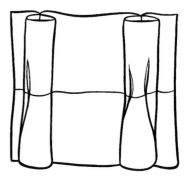

Cartridge pleats

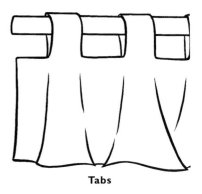

Tabs

Eyelets

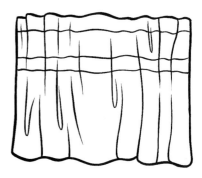

Cased heading

(Almost) Instant Curtains

Armed with a length of heading tape, you can quickly transform a rich variety of attractive textiles into unusual and stylish curtains with almost no sewing involved. Try tablecloths or bedspreads, for example, (in cotton lace or colourful checks), antique linen sheets (or new, crisp cotton ones), traditional quilts, cosy chenille throws, soft wool and cotton blankets, flat-weave rugs, or even pretty shawls or lengths of vibrant saris. Use them in pairs to create a set of conventional curtains, or singly to make a simple panel.

With heavier items such as rugs and quilts, you are really restricted to pieces that are roughly the right length. You can cheat a little here, though, by linking two rows of rings together at the top to gain a few centimetres or allowing any excess fabric to trail slightly onto the floor. Lightweight textiles, however (especially those that are the same on both sides), are much more adaptable. Choose something, perhaps a lace tablecloth, that is significantly longer than your window. (If the window measures 2 m [7 ft], your curtain should be at least 230 cm [90.5 in]). Sew your heading tape to the back at a distance from the top that is equal to the excess length. When the curtain is hung, the excess will gently flop over at the front to form a graceful pelmet.

For an even simpler, completely no-sew option, forget heading tape and hooks altogether and use a set of metal curtain clips: the ones that hook onto conventional rings or those that incorporate a ring in their own shape so they can slot over the curtain pole. They both work by gripping the fabric in a strong spring in the same way as a bulldog clip. Curtain clips come in several different finishes (brass, chrome, black, etc.), weights and designs, although none of them are strong enough to hold heavy fabric and lining. They are ideal, however, for cotton, linen and lace, and for covering small windows with appealing (and also inexpensive) household textiles such as colourful tea towels, embroidered tray cloths and large table napkins, perhaps used as café curtains.

Opposite: For the ultimate in instant curtains, drape a pair of gold-threaded sari lengths over a slim pole.

This page: Simple sprung clips anchor a sheer fabric panel in position so its woven edge trims a neat self-pelmet.

blinds

Although much depends on individual characteristics, blinds tend to look more at home in spare or architectural rooms than softer, more organic ones. Most of them can be fitted outside or inside the window recess, using brackets fixed to the top of the reveal (top-fix), or at each side (side-fix). Many popular styles can be custom made in the material and size of your choice, and some blinds are sold in a range of stock sizes as well (choose the size closest to your window). If you particularly enjoy sewing, consider making your own fabric blinds. Any good soft-furnishing manual will provide detailed instructions.

Roller blinds

Roller blinds consist of a panel of fabric fixed to a sprung, wooden roller that allows you to extend the blind to any length you want and then tug it gently to rewind it. You can easily make these blinds using a proprietary kit but if you decide to do this, avoid using thick fabrics and those with pile, ribbing or any kind of raised trim that will prevent them from rolling up again smoothly.

Roman blinds

When lowered, Roman blinds also present a flat panel of fabric, but they fold up into neatly stacked pleats. They are made by passing cords through rows of rings or eyelets fitted to the back of the fabric. These cords are pulled to raise the blind, then wound around a wall-fixed cleat to anchor it. Roman blinds are just as easy to make as roller blinds, but they are more of a sewing project than a DIY exercise.

London blinds

A toned-down version of the frilly festoon blind, London blinds are constructed in much the same way as Roman blinds, but instead of forming horizontal pleats, they draw up into a set of gentle gathers. When lowered, they also become a virtually flat panel rather than the rows of ruched swags typical of festoon blinds. London blinds are not usually available ready made; you either need to make them yourself or have them sewn to order.

Venetian blinds

Made from aluminium, plastic or wood, the horizontal slats that form a traditional Venetian blind are operated by means of corded tapes that run down both sides. The whole blind can be pulled completely clear of the window, lowered to cover it completely or adjusted to admit varying degrees of light according to the angle of the slats.

Vertical louvre blinds

Instead of being pulled up from the bottom in the traditional way, vertical louvre blinds are drawn to one side on a system of corded pulleys, much like a single curtain. In addition, they can be pivoted to control the light in the same way as Venetian blinds. Wide slats, made from either stiffened fabric, wood or metal, give these blinds a strongly institutional feel and they are a popular choice for office windows. Most vertical louvre blinds are used to cover large windows and they must be made to measure by a specialist manufacturer.

Roll-up blinds

This very basic construction is used for many off-the-peg blinds: those made from cane and bamboo, for example, thin wooden slats or reeds (pinoleum blinds) and paper. All of these blinds are drawn up by means of a cord-and-pulley system. Roll-up fabric blinds are among the very easiest to make yourself. If you don't need to draw them up and down regularly, you can even do without the pulley system – just roll (or gather) them up to the required height and then anchor them in position with lengths of strong tape.

Opposite: The roller blind at its most charmingly traditional (top): with hemmed sides, a wide lace border and a wooden acorn to pull it up and down. In a room where simple shapes and neutral hues set the scene (below), Roman blinds in natural linen are the ideal choice.

Left: Wide slats of honey-coloured wood transform the faintly institutional look of a standard metal Venetian blind.

shutters,
screens & panels

Wooden shutters, screens and panels, whether left in their natural finish or given a coat of satin-finish paint, offer visual warmth and classic charm, combined with clean lines.

Solid panel shutters

The formal windows of many eighteenth- and nineteenth-century town houses were fitted with tall hinged shutters, many of which are still in place today, tidily folded away into deep purpose-built recesses on either side of the window frame. These somewhat imposing (and also very secure) window coverings, often fitted with iron bars to anchor them neatly into place, are known as solid panel shutters. If you are lucky enough to inherit an original set, it may be worth having them restored to working order. Otherwise, consider installing new shutters. They can either be custom-made using traditional materials and methods by a specialist firm of carpenters or improvised by an enthusiastic amateur from two or more hinged timber panels or sheets of plywood, hardboard or MDF cut to size.

Louvred shutters

Available in stock sizes or made to measure, louvred (sometimes known as plantation) shutters operate in exactly the same way as those with solid panels. Unlike solid shutters, however, they admit light through a row of central slats, which are either fixed in position or adjustable, like those on Venetian blinds. In style terms, louvred shutters are a particularly good way of suggesting a colonial influence, but they can also adapt readily to a wide range of contemporary and traditional schemes.

Screens

When it comes to window coverings, the term 'screen' usually means a single hardwood frame containing a central panel of flat or gathered fabric, paper (like Japanese shoji screens) or strips of timber arranged in a grid or lattice motif. Some screens consist of a sheet of hardboard or plywood that has been pierced to filter the light in intricate patterns. A screen can be designed to cover either an entire window or just the bottom half. It may be fixed in position, hinged to open in the manner of a door or even fitted with a sliding track or rail.

TOP TIPS

1 Install two-tier (known as tier-on-tier) shutters, which allow you to cover the window completely, leave it clear or close just the bottom half, letting light pour in at the top. A fixed, half-height screen would act in the same way as café curtains to fulfil a similar function.

2 To achieve the same effect as a conventional window treatment without fixing anything in place, invest in a hinged, floor-standing screen that stands in front of the window at night. During the day, it can be moved to one side or folded away. This idea is particularly useful for those in short-term or rented accommodation who are reluctant to invest in furnishings they can't take away with them.

Left: Plain tier-on-tier shutters offer maximum flexibility combined with the purity of line this cool, calm bedroom demands.

Right: Create the effect of stained glass with X-film gel, a transparent, self-adhesive acetate used by photographers to tint their lighting. Here, each window pane is covered with cut-out stripes arranged in neat parallel lines.

Panels

Where privacy is of paramount importance (in bathrooms, for example), or the view is so unpleasant that your wisest option is to block it out permanently, consider replacing some or all of your original window panes with opaque or translucent panels. These can take the form of mirror glass, frosted glass (or perspex) or coloured glass, which is available in solid sheets or pretty, multi-hued patterns. To create a similar look with much less effort and expense, experiment with etching spray for an authentically textured look (often used in conjunction with small stencils), or sheets of coloured acetate or tracing paper cut to size and tacked in place with spray adhesive.

LIGHTING

Badly lit rooms can lower your spirits. They are also hard to work, read or even relax in, and they give a cheerless, unflattering cast to all your furnishings, and very probably to your complexion as well.

Lighting is not a scary, specialist subject that only architects and designers can really understand. The basic guidelines are very simple, so armed with these and a practical approach, you will soon be able to improve both the look and overall atmosphere of your home dramatically. There are two main categories of lighting and two secondary ones. The most important types are ambient (sometimes called background) lighting and task lighting, while the supporting players are accent lighting and decorative lighting.

ambient lighting

One of the most common culprits when it comes to creating bleak, shadowless spaces is the ubiquitous ceiling pendant. The problem is inherent not just in this fitting, but in the way it's expected to fulfil so many different functions when its scope is so limited. Ambient, background or mood lighting should bathe a room with warm and subtle general illumination and eliminate any harsh contrasts between strongly lit working areas and the spaces around them. During the day, natural light is often enough, but at night you'll have to fall back on artificial illumination in the form of table, wall or floor (often called 'standard') lights, recessed ceiling fixtures or adjustable track systems. These can be switched on individually or wired into the same circuit so you can turn on all the lights in one room with a single switch. For maximum flexibility, fit dimmer switches to individual fittings or to whole circuits so you can instantly adjust the brightness of the room.

task lighting

As the name suggests, task lamps are used to concentrate light on a specific activity such as working on a computer. To be effective, they require a bulb of at least 60 watts, but some people need even more brightness. Experiment until you find the most comfortable level for you! Too much light (or any glare) can cause as much discomfort as too little. Remember, too, that eyes weaken with age and a 40-year-old will need three times more light than a 10-year-old to see just as well. The best task lamps are adjustable (like a spotlight, Anglepoise or classic gooseneck), so you can focus the beam exactly where you need it. When your work is done, you can angle the light towards the wall to provide extra ambient illumination.

accent lighting

This category covers any light fittings that are intended to highlight a particular object or feature in a room: picture lights, for instance, or spotlights that are focussed on an exotic plant or an attractive collection of china or glass. It has to

To make the best of an existing ceiling pendant, disguise it with a novelty shade made from plastic discs that filter the light in psychedelic patterns. If you're troubled with glare from the bulb, however, either fit a reflector spot or choose a shade that covers the bulb completely, like a classic paper globe. Choose a bamboo frame in preference to a wire one, and reinforce its oriental charm by going for one of the larger sizes.

TOP TIPS

1 Light bulbs always die at the least convenient moment, so put aside a supply of spares – especially the ones not widely available in supermarkets or convenience stores.

2 Low-energy light bulbs are more costly than ordinary ones, but they produce much stronger illumination in relation to their wattage and they last up to ten times longer. Best of all, they use 80 per cent less energy than standard light bulbs.

3 If you're trying to get by with single ceiling pendants, explore the alternatives by taking two or three table lamps into each room. Turn them on and then switch off the central main light to experience the dramatic effect this has on the atmosphere in the room.

4 Pale neutral lampshades (white, cream, parchment, etc.) are the best choice for all domestic fittings. Coloured shades have a tendency to distort light, and dark ones (fabric or card) limit it significantly.

5 Unless you're trying for a specific theatrical or high-camp look, avoid coloured light bulbs and those shaped like flames. While you're building up your decorating confidence, stick to simple and honest effects rather than poor imitations of something else.

be said, though, that rooms can be wonderfully stylish without any accent lighting at all, so unless you have a feature that you really want to draw attention to, you can probably do without it.

decorative lighting

Under this heading comes any fitting that is valued more for looks than usefulness: twinkly fairylights, coloured fluorescent tubes resembling space-age weapons, huge, glowing spheres like radio-active balloons, and those ultimate kitsch classics: lava lamps. Candles and real fires are essentially decorative lights as well (unless you're in the middle of a power cut), but some pundits slot them into a separate category – kinetic (moving) lighting.

Above: This understated architectural floor lamp provides plenty of illumination for reading, yet swivels toward the flawless white wall, washing it with an ambient glow. To change the mood completely, it can also spotlight the languid twentieth-century portrait nearby.

LIGHT SOURCES

There are three main types of light bulb or 'lamp', to use the correct term:

- **Tungsten filament** lamps (conventional household bulbs) are the most common type. They come in clear, pearl and coloured versions, and their illumination has a warm, slightly yellowish cast. Cheap to use, they give off an appealing glow (left), but as they burn out comparatively quickly, they are not energy efficient. Because tungsten filament lamps generate considerable heat, shades made from paper, fabric or plastic should not be positioned too close to them.

- **Fluorescent lamps** usually take the form of tubes that give off a cooler light than any tungsten source. Despite the recent development of 'warm' ranges, their colour rendering tends to be distorted and many people find them too harsh and uncomfortable. Their most common domestic use is for concealed lighting. Fluorescent lamps use energy very efficiently, though, and they last much longer than conventional tungsten lamps.

- **Tungsten halogen** lamps are much smaller than either of the other two, yet they produce clear, strong illumination that is closer to natural light than any other artificial source. They are also the most expensive of the three types of lamp.

CHOOSING FURNITURE

The furniture that you start out with is likely to be a mixture of items you already own, those passed on by well-meaning friends and relatives, junk-shop or boot fair finds and brand-new purchases. Wherever it comes from, though, avoid letting any furnishings through your door that don't feel absolutely right for you and your home. Once you've begun to weave your own look with colours, shapes and surfaces, it's easy to spoil the overall effect by amassing a collection of ill-assorted bits and pieces that (if you're honest about it), you've taken on board largely because they're sturdy and serviceable – and possibly cheap, or even free.

However, the cost is high in terms of creating style and atmosphere, especially since you can easily get by at first with just somewhere to sleep, a comfortable place to relax (even if it's simply a selection of squashy cushions piled up on the floor), a table to write and serve meals on, and some basic provision for storage. Everything else can be added gradually as you discover what you need, and find (or are able to afford) the things you really love.

explore the options

Even if your rooms are small, don't be afraid to use large pieces of furniture. One or two dramatic items – a sofa or table that spans one end of a narrow room, perhaps, or a huge chest of drawers that fills a wide alcove – make a bold and stylish impression, as well as being hugely useful. On the other hand, a collection of dinky tables, chairs and shelves is a much less practical solution and has the capacity to make even big spaces appear cramped and cluttered.

Be careful, too, of apparently ingenious dual-purpose designs: coffee tables that can be converted into dining tables; stools that open out into single beds and cupboards containing fold-down work surfaces, for example. They are only worthwhile if the item in question performs all of its functions efficiently, it is easy to operate, and you aren't planning to put it through its paces every day. Otherwise, the

Above: Simple upholstered cubes provide extra seating and surfaces, and they will adapt easily for use in other rooms or future schemes.

Opposite: These versatile chairs in rich mock suede are stylish enough for the living room, yet fit neatly around the dining table to accommodate guests.

TOP TIPS

1 Before you start to look for a particular item, take accurate measurements of the space you have in mind for it (plus any relevant access areas). This is particularly vital when choosing custom-made pieces such as upholstered seating, which can't be returned at a later stage, or those you hope to find in an antique shop or flea market or to buy at auction. Keep these measurements with you so that when you see something you really like you'll know instantly if you have room for it. If you have to go home and measure first then you run the risk of losing out to another buyer.

2 Depending on your tastes, search for genuinely old items of furniture (antique or second-hand, according to your budget), modern pieces or new furniture that continue to be made using traditional methods and materials, such as a pine table with simple turned legs or a sprung chesterfield sofa. Reproduction pieces employing mass-production techniques and inferior materials to imitate (often inaccurately) the shapes and detailing of genuine period designs have absolutely no place in stylish rooms.

novelty is likely to wear off rapidly as you start to become weary of the hassle, and the extra money it cost will be wasted. The best multi-purpose items are always the simplest: a blanket box that doubles up as a side table, perhaps, or a single divan covered with a cosy throw to provide extra seating.

buying second-hand

Ferreting through junk shops, flea markets and charity shops is one of the great joys of furnishing your first home, and if you become hooked on this particular pursuit, it is likely to remain a life-long pleasure. When it comes to furniture, look for solidly constructed items in classic shapes or quirkily styled in a way that suits your look. Don't worry too much about broken handles, loose joints or scratched paint – these things are fairly easy and inexpensive to put right once you get them home. Unless you're very sure of what you're taking on, however, avoid upholstery that needs re-springing, chair seats or backs that have to be re-caned, polished wood that requires re-finishing, or decorative metalwork that needs replacing since these are all highly skilled tasks that require specialist training and extensive practice, and are therefore extremely costly to commission.

Similarly, if you fall in love with an old bath or basin, seek confirmation that it's in full working order with no cracks in the porcelain or chips to the enamel before you buy – or reconcile yourself to a hefty bill for re-finishing. Above all, beware of woodworm: a sprinkling of small holes in any piece of timber should put you immediately on your guard. Either pass it up or make sure it's been treated properly before you give it house room.

flexibility & function

Try to clear your mind of any furnishing preconceptions you may already have and look at every piece that appeals to you with a fresh eye. For example, as well as storing socks and sweaters in the bedroom, a chest of drawers can be used to hold paperwork, collections of CDs, videos or DVDs and board games in the living room; household linen, utensils and small items of equipment in the kitchen; gloves, scarves, bags and hats in the hall, or even toiletries and clean towels in the bathroom. If you see a shapely old wardrobe for sale at a reasonable price, consider painting it and putting in a row of shelves to turn it into a capacious kitchen cupboard. Use a mantel mirror as a headboard, a redundant pew or a garden bench for extra seating, a slatted metal plant or baker's stand as a shelving unit, or an ancient sink as a planter. Some items – a stylish folding screen, for instance, or a wooden chest – are so useful and adaptable that you will use them constantly until they fall apart.

Although this way of thinking opens up a whole area of decorative exploration, it can be taken too far. For example, unspeakable acts of vandalism include turning heirloom jugs or vases into lamp bases and drilling holes in an antique cabinet to accommodate a television set and VCR.

alternative sources

As well as searching through markets and junk shops for things that inspire you, widen your shopping base to take in office furnishers (look out for filing and storage cabinets, plans chests, occasional chairs and folding tables); catering suppliers (for shelving units and hanging racks, as well as china, glass and utensils); shop fitters (for clothing rails, cupboards, mirrors and funky display gear), and hospital equipment specialists (for trolleys and folding metal-framed screens). Often these industrial designs offer classic appeal and solid, pared-down practicality at considerably lower prices than you'll ever see in trendy furnishing stores. If possible, try to acquire catalogues from a few of these outlets or visit their websites first so that you can check out ranges at leisure. Half the fun of this lies in finding new functions for old favourites: a brightly coloured locker or filing cabinet can be used to store clothes and shoes, perhaps, and a hospital trolley may accommodate all the stationery in your home office.

If you live anywhere near an architectural salvage yard, make a point of dropping in on a regular basis to see what's available. Apart from structural items such as interesting doors and period fireplaces, many of them also carry a fascinating assortment of furnishing treasures all rescued from about-to-be-demolished banks, shops, office buildings, theatres, schools, hospitals and ancient churches, as well as residential properties.

Above left: An old commercial fitting designed to hold retail stock, office supplies or industrial parts is perfect for jewellery, make-up and accessories. It would be equally useful in the kitchen for storing cutlery, utensils, dried herbs and tea towels.

Left: Stripped and limed to emphasize their pale wood grain, two furnishing survivors from an earlier age provide visual interest in this stark white room. Note the simple cantilevered shelf that holds a constantly changing display of pictures and objects.

DESIGN DETAILS

Rooms, like people, have a tendency to inspire instant reactions. To some degree, the elements we respond to most strongly, whether positively or negatively, are dominant and obvious: the overall colour scheme, the floor covering or the specific type of furniture. Almost as significant, however, are the subtle touches that, almost before we're aware of them, are helping to define the aesthetic atmosphere. 'God,' declared the iconic twentieth-century architect Ludwig Mies van der Rohe, 'is in the details'.

hardware & electrics

In the same way that upmarket shoes or a good haircut can make chain-store clothes look more expensive, well-designed and appropriate domestic hardware, such as door knobs, power sockets and light switches, can give the most ordinary room the kind of slick finish that makes it special.

As it is almost part of the fabric of a building, the hardware you choose should have some visual affinity with it. This does not necessarily mean it has to match exactly in date and style, but uncomfortable contrasts should be avoided. In a period house or flat, for example, consider replacing cheap,

plastic switches and sockets with plain brass (switches also come with hardwood plates), and rejecting mass-produced, lever-operated door handles and locks in favour of proper door knobs. These are also available in brass, plain china or even Victorian-style cut glass. You can sometimes track down antique door furniture (try junk shops, boot fairs, markets and antique shops), but most specialist retailers sell new ranges in traditional shapes. Stick to the plainest ones.

In modern buildings, white plastic switches and sockets don't jar quite as much, but they are still easy – and remarkably cheap – to improve on: change them for similar models in bright colours or, if your style is cool and architectural, go for aluminium. Door furniture can take the form of tough, nylon-plastic lever handles, again in vivid colours, or sleekly styled levers or cylindrical knobs in brushed aluminium.

handles & pulls

Give an interesting and individual look to your storage furniture by replacing any dull, dated or damaged handles with smart, new ones. There are plenty of exciting alternatives available in shops and mail-order catalogues (especially those specializing in imported goods), including both conventional designs (look for brass, china, chrome or cut-glass resembling huge, semi-precious stones) and wittily themed shapes like rolling-pin handles for the kitchen, fish knobs for the bathroom and giant button drawer pulls for the bedroom). Try making your own pulls from smooth pebbles or large shells gathered from the beach, or use wooden spoons or old-fashioned dolly-type clothes pegs as drawer handles. This kind of imaginative detailing can quickly transform any new, but characterless items of furniture or junk-shop pieces you decide to restore.

For anyone who is intent on creating a truly minimalist environment, there is, of course, only one conceivable type of opening device: an invisible one. To leave the exterior visually uninterrupted, fit cupboard doors with a push-spring mechanism, while drawers should have a finger recess underneath.

cords & flexes

If the standard-issue cable on your freestanding light fittings lets you down in the style stakes, change it. Specialist suppliers sell flex on the roll in several different designs: try silky, plaited flex in period rooms, plain brown or black flex (slightly more unassuming than the white version), or curly flex which comes in a range of colours. When you need length, this is always a far neater solution than tangled, trailing straight flex, and you're less likely to trip over it. For the same reasons, choose curly extension leads rather than conventional ones.

Some ceiling lights, especially those in bathrooms, are operated by pull cords, most of which have nasty bits of plastic at the end. Improve on the existing cord by replacing it with ribbon, strung beads, fine chain or a length of tasselled rope, like one end of a tie-back. At very least, get rid of the plastic pull and replace it with something more exciting: a carved wooden acorn perhaps, an unusual metal or resin pull, a predrilled shell or pebble, or a giant bead or button.

Clockwise, from far left: Switch plates in chrome and brass, door knobs made from brushed aluminium and novelty light pulls in naturalistic or abstract shapes all add individuality and interest to your rooms.

accessories

The minor decorative elements in each of your rooms play a huge part in the final look: they provide a necessary change of scale from larger pieces of furniture and the expansive surfaces of the floor, walls and ceiling, and offer huge scope not only for expressing your individuality, but also for playing off one colour, surface or shape against another. Accessories and accent pieces also make it possible to create fresh, new looks without any major upheaval, by replacing or revamping them – or even just moving them around later.

TEXTILES

Smaller soft-furnishing details, such as cushions and throws, not only give a room visual warmth and softness, they also make it much more comfortable and inviting. It's not enough, though, to gather together a motley collection of textiles acquired as gifts or purchased impulsively. To establish a sense of cohesion, ensure that all the materials involved complement one another. Likewise, make your cushions the same (or a very similar) size. For maximum support and dramatic effect, go for jumbo feather pads

instead of small, conventional ones. Cut (or order) covers a little smaller than the pad in each case to give plumper contours to your finished cushions.

LAMPS & CANDLES

Here again, don't settle for dull or undersized lamps and shades. Go for strong style statements (try spheres, cubes or columns in metal, ceramic, paper or wood), industrial spots or bright, quirky designs. If you're not sure how to choose a shade, head for a specialist retailer and ask for advice.

To cast your rooms in a matchlessly beguiling glow, invest in a collection of candles: creamy church candles or plain, white ones (perhaps clustered together on a large plate, platter or tray) always look stylish and classy, whereas decorated, coloured or novelty designs lose their charm once they have started to burn down. Remember, too, that coloured wax stains indelibly, so any that drips on a tablecloth will case problems. Finally, unless you're setting a formal table, go for chunky column or cube candles rather than slender ones: they make a much better overall display and also produce a far more consistent, longer-lasting flame.

SCREENS

When you're trying to accommodate several different functions in every room and maintain an impression of effortless calm and immaculate taste at the same time, you could scarcely make a wiser investment than a folding screen. From the wide range available (including those made from plywood panels, gathered or stretched fabric, or softboard sheets that act as giant pinboards), choose one that suits your look and use it to define space and restore order where it's needed: in the bedroom to conceal a hand basin or a mound of ironing, perhaps, or in the living room to hide the television or to divide a room off to accommodate a house guest in complete privacy.

TREASURES, COLLECTIONS & CLUTTER

It's easy to allow all the surfaces in your home – the coffee table, shelves, chest of drawers and fridge – to become completely covered with things: from objects you genuinely love and enjoy looking at to domestic debris such as coins, cards and keys. To stem this flow before it gets out of hand, install a roomy and presentable container to hold everything that falls into the second category. Choose a huge bowl, perhaps, or a wicker basket, and get into the habit of using it as your daily dumping ground.

Try not to put anything on display simply because it was given to you, or you can't decide what else to do with it. Edit your treasures down to those you can't live without, then maximize their impact by grouping them according to purpose (jugs, perfume bottles or ink stands), pattern (tartan, tortoiseshell or animal print), or theme (fish, trains or Mickey Mouse), rather than dotting them around the room.

Far left: Keep major design elements simple and use striking materials and unusual textures as accents.

Above left: Thousands of tiny glass beads give these tasselled pendant shades their exotic allure.

Left: This folding screen has glass panels that lift out so you can display your favourite images in the squares.

- To find original works of art that won't require a second mortgage, investigate the degree shows at your local art school. If you see something you like, ask how you can contact the artist.
- Buy a collection of empty frames (clip frames are the cheapest) and fill them with linked images that cost next to nothing: fruit or sweet wrappers, for example, printed beer mats, paperback book covers, theatre programmes, lace collars, and so on.
- Create a similar display using deep box frames filled with pebbles, shells, combs, letter openers, badges or bottle tops.
- Instead of a static image, fix a large, hanging grid or pinboard (made from metal, fabric-covered cork or a section of cheap garden trellis) on which you can create a constantly changing display of postcards and photographs.
- As well as framed images, hang a collection of shallow baskets or trays, straw hats, pretty plates (but not valuable ones since the hanging mechanism can cause damage), or beaded handbags.
- Turn an area rug, a small quilt, an embroidered throw or a length of beautiful fabric into a luxurious hanging that dominates your room.

pictures, hangings
& wall displays

Unless you've inherited a fabulous collection of art, at some stage you're likely to feel intimidated by vast expanses of blank wall — however partial you are to the minimalist, pared-down look. When this feeling strikes, hold on to the thought that it's always better to leave walls blank and wait to discover the images that you really like, rather than to put up boring or indifferent prints or posters simply to fill the space up quickly.

STRENGTH IN NUMBERS

If you already have a few images — whether photographs, prints or paintings — that you want to display, try to find an attractive way of grouping them together instead of spreading them around the room, each one marooned in a vast, plaster sea. As long as they have a basic visual sympathy (that is, they don't contrast violently in size or style), your pictures will make a stronger impression and your room will appear more balanced. Groups of pictures should always share one common plane, so align them across the top, through the middle or along the bottom. If they're all the same size, a formal grid or a straight line

TOP TIPS

1 If you have an old-fashioned picture rail, try hanging pictures from it using lengths of chain and strong hooks that slot over the moulding. This system not only adds decorative interest, it is also extremely practical since no damage is inflicted on the walls and the pictures can be moved about as often as you like.

2 To display a quilt, rug or fabric hanging, sew a length of curtain heading tape, a row of tabs or loops or a wide casing at the back and suspend it from a slim pole or a length of garden cane. Alternatively, attach a thin, timber batten to the wall (make it less conspicuous by painting it to match first), and then screw in a row of cup hooks that correspond directly to ties or loops carefully stitched along the top of the hanging.

3 Choosing a mount and frame for a treasured image is a complex task. Unless you're very sure of what you want, find a specialist framer and take your picture in at a quiet time so the staff have time to explain all the options to you.

treatment works best; when they differ in height, stagger them city-skyline fashion instead of placing them in strict ascending or descending order. Whatever effect you're aiming for, play around with several arrangements on the floor before you settle on the one you like best and commit yourself to it by filling your wall with holes.

IN PLAIN VIEW

Most people have a tendency to place their pictures too high on the wall, especially as they are very often viewed from a sitting position. Aim to position pictures at your own eye level, unless you're hanging something over a piece of furniture like a sofa, bed or desk, in which case it should be placed near enough to look connected.

Don't be afraid to let your pictures dominate the space they occupy; try almost-filling a small wall or an alcove with one big picture, poster or wall hanging, for example, or a group of smaller items hung very close together with only a narrow border around the outside. A series of small pictures of the same size work well in a line or geometric arrangement.

Above: Grouped in long, slim horizontal frames and hung low for maximum impact, these snapshot-sized floral studies reflect their owner's ruling passion.

Opposite: Parallel rows of tiny glass shelves provide almost invisible support for a three-dimensional display of exquisite white-on-white evening bags.

flowers & plants

Whether they're trailing and leafy, tall and spiky, delicate and pale, or languid and exotic, fresh flowers and healthy plants always provide a universally appealing display and (especially in built-up areas) a welcome reminder of a real garden's tranquil pleasures.

Like small pictures or single ornaments, however, isolated and insignificant houseplants and skimpy posies tend to get lost in the comparatively large and hectic visual landscape of your rooms. If possible, go for large, lush plants or sculptural, floor-standing specimens (a lavender bush perhaps, a prickly cactus or a lofty Swiss cheese plant). Alternatively, group together several pots of the same plant, such as ivy, geranium or busy lizzie, to create a verdant spectacle. Try trailing them over the edge of a shelf perhaps, suspending them from a row of hooks or placing them in front of a window to filter the light prettily.

Use the kitchen window-sill as a miniature herb garden so you can have a constant (and very decorative) supply of parsley, chives and mint. There's no need to organize special containers for your houseplants, but try to replace unattractive plastic pots with terracotta ones, which look much nicer and cost very little.

In the same way, go for low-cost, seasonal flowers such as daffodils, stocks or tulips that you can afford to buy in bulk, rather than meagre assortments of expensive hot-house blooms. No elaborate and exotic floral arrangement makes a more powerful impact than a huge bunch of identical flowers artlessly massed in a single glass or earthenware container. Alternatively, place single stems of brightly coloured flowers like gerberas in simple glasses and group them together.

Out of season, experiment with a profusion of forced hyacinths or paperwhites (both of which are intoxicatingly fragrant) by filling a huge pot or a simple china basin with their bulbs. If you're feeling adventurous, experiment with a range of low-key containers for your flowers and plants: graceful jugs and bowls, utilitarian florists' buckets or watering cans in galvanized metal, and rustic woven baskets with waterproof containers hidden inside them, as well as traditional purpose-designed vases, boxes and tubs. Remember, though, that highly decorated designs in garish colours and fussy shapes are much harder to use successfully since they tend to wage an aesthetic battle with their contents.

TOP TIPS

1 Never place flowers or plants on or near a television set, a sound system, a computer or any other item of electrical equipment. It takes only a single drop of water or misdirected spray to cause serious damage.

2 If you enjoy having growing things around but your time, skill and horticultural knowledge are all limited, choose plants that will survive with less-than-ideal treatment. The seductively lacy fronds of a maidenhair fern, for example, will soon resemble a sisal doormat if you don't know how to look after it.

3 Look for cut flowers that are not yet fully opened. When still in bud, they have a charm of their own and when they do come out, they will last a lot longer than full-blown blooms.

4 Some common houseplants help to clear chemical pollutants, such as formaldehyde and benzene, from the air. *Chlorophytum* (spider plant) and *philodendron* (sweetheart plant) are particularly useful in this way.

Left: Cultivate your own herb garden in a collection of matching miniature flower pots. These are made of cast aluminium with engraved numerals, but plain terracotta ones are equally stylish.

Right: This towering, sculptural arrangement of dried, tendril-like branches looks stylish and expensive, yet cost nothing. In common with the fresh flowers and pussy willows nearby, it is displayed in a clear glass container that doesn't compete for attention.

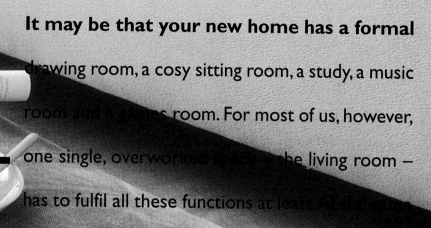

4

It may be that your new home has a formal drawing room, a cosy sitting room, a study, a music room and a games room. For most of us, however, one single, overworked space — the living room — has to fulfil all these functions at least. At the same

living

spaces

time, we also expect it to be comfortable and convenient, and to look ordered and stylish. This weighty brief is unlikely to be met by chance, so give yourself a head start by taking stock early on of all the activities you want to accommodate here: conventional ones like reading, entertaining and watching television, and more specialized ones such as working from home.

PLANNING

Even (and perhaps especially) if your living room needs to cater for a vast and diverse number of activities, its primary role will be to offer a comfortable place to relax — for one or two people every day, and for larger numbers when you entertain. Here, the most important consideration is seating: the right kind (upholstered, occasional), the right size (large sofa, small sofa, chairs), and the right amount to complement your room.

Consider other vital elements such as tables next. Will you need a dining table — and if so, how many people do you want it to seat? Do you do a lot of paperwork at home or spend hours sorting out a photograph collection? How much surface area do you need for displaying groups of framed photographs, plants, vases, ornaments, etc., and how much is required for practical items such as table lamps?

Storage is the next major requirement. The key questions to be asked are: 'What kind?' and 'How much?'. Do you have an extensive library or just a dozen paperbacks? A playlist-size stack of CDs or a few greatest hits collections? A home-cinema stock of films on video or last year's blockbusters only?

As well as subtle background illumination, how much task lighting will you need? Perhaps a floor lamp or angled spot near your reading chair or an adjustable desk that fits on the table where you write letters and pay bills?

bringing it all together

Once you have established the main elements of your scheme (those you already have and the ones you intend to acquire), you can begin to plan their arrangement. The optimum layout for a room is not always the one that seems the most obvious. For example, many people are convinced that furniture has to be lined up along the walls, waiting-room fashion, but this arrangement often looks awkward and makes poor use of space, so try to explore all the alternatives. In many living rooms the most dominant item is the sofa, so start by establishing its position. The best place for such a bulky item might be up against a wall, but it could also look wonderful in the middle of the room, facing a working fireplace or a window with a particularly inspiring aspect. If the floor stretches out like a glorified corridor, this awkwardness will be accentuated by positioning the sofa on one of the longer walls. Placed at right angles, the sofa will not only correct the shape of the room visually; it can also divide it into separate activity areas — living and dining, perhaps. You can also use a freestanding bookcase or an imposing storage chest in the same way. Once the sofa is in place, arrange your other upholstered pieces nearby, bearing in mind that people tend to feel most comfortable conversing with someone who is sitting at right angles to them. The next best arrangement is face to face, and the least satisfactory one is side by side.

For convenience and safety's sake, make sure there's a surface of some kind near every easy chair or sofa. Cups, glasses, plates and ashtrays left on the floor can easily be knocked over. Another important safety tip is to place the dining table, especially if it's in everyday use, as near to

Opposite: Like a big, bright sun, an unusual round rug establishes the colour theme, defines the conversation area and reinforces the fresh, modern style of this light-filled, airy space.

This page: Walls subtly colourwashed with mellow ochre and a graceful daybed upholstered in crimson velvet set the scene in this supremely inviting room.

the kitchen as possible. The greater the distance and the more obstacles there are between kitchen and table, the more likely it is that the food – or even the cook – will end up on the floor. On the other hand, if the table is used only occasionally for eating, but regularly as a desk, a more sensible decision may be to position it to take advantage of the light from a large window.

Look carefully at how the different elements in the room relate to one another. An inspired storage solution for the television, for example, is of no value if the screen is not clearly visible from most of the comfortable seats. In a household with more than one person, a home-office area may be seriously compromised if it's on a main traffic path, say between the sofa and the kitchen.

schemes & surfaces

Because your living room is likely to be occupied for longer periods and also used to accommodate more activities and objects than any other area, it is not the place to express your wackiest design fantasies. Keep the colours warm, inviting and seductive, and the decorating tricks to a minimum.

Heavy-traffic areas like this one call for durable flooring to cope with stains and tracked-in dirt. If possible, the flooring should carry straight through from the adjoining entrance hall or corridor. Wooden floors certainly qualify in terms of practicality, but if you want the softness, warmth and sound insulation that only carpet can provide, choose a hard-wearing weave in a medium (rather than a very pale) shade. In either case, invest in a small rug to protect the most vulnerable patch in front of the sofa and to define the central seating area at the same time.

Living room windows are often the largest and most formal ones in any flat or house, so the treatment you choose for them plays a proportionally greater part in the whole scheme. While it's not a good idea to skimp on the curtain rail or track, or the quality and fullness of the fabric, you may still be able to get away without using any lining here since dimming the glare of the early morning sun is much less vital in this room than in the bedroom.

changing scenes

It's important to be quite flexible in your ideas because when you've lived with your room for a while, you may find that you want to make a few alterations to it. Some arrangements, for example, may not work out as well as you'd originally hoped, while others fill needs you didn't expect. Similarly, some colours that look terrific on the sample card take on a totally different cast when they're actually on the wall and viewed at different times of the day and evening. From time to time, too, your life will change a little: perhaps you'll entertain more or take on extra work at home. Being prepared to re-arrange things occasionally will not only make your home a much more efficient space to live in, it will also provide you with a refreshing change of scene.

SEATING

If, like most people, you associate the living room with leisurely hours, gentler pursuits and a relaxed frame of mind, one of your first furnishing priorities is likely to be a welcoming, comfortable sofa. Upholstered seating is one of those areas where cost and quality matter a great deal. Downmarket designs are padded with foam or synthetic wadding and their cushions are supported on rubber straps or long, zigzag springs stretched horizontally across a flimsy frame. Solidly made sofas and chairs have a hardwood frame, traditional coil springing, thick padding built up from layers of fibre, horsehair and felt, and cushions stuffed with either the best feathers or a superior man-made substitute. Well-made upholstery looks better, it's more comfortable to sit on, it offers more support and it lasts longer. Cheaper items soon wear out with daily use and become lumpy and saggy. The key here is to make a positive choice: if all you want is something bright, smart and comparatively short term, go for one of the colourful ranges offered at irresistibly low prices in chain stores. If you expect your seating to last for years, however, you'll have to pay more.

In terms of shape and style, bear in mind the sitting position you find most comfortable, as well as the way you'd like your seating to look. If you want support behind your head, go for a high back but if you like to drape yourself over the sides of a sofa, choose one with a low, wide back and arms. Alternatively, if you prefer to prop yourself up at one end with your feet stretched out, using your sofa like a glorified chaise longue, you'll appreciate high, well-padded arms. Similarly, very tall people should look for deep seats (i.e. longer from front to back), whereas those of a more modest stature can find their feet dangling off the floor unless the depth is scaled down accordingly. Low seating gives a sleek, contemporary feel to any room and increases the impression of height, but it's much more awkward to get in and out of, so keep this in mind if you have any mobility problems (or any regular visitors who suffer in this way).

When it comes to size, take into account the number of guests you hope to accommodate in your living room, as well as its dimensions. Remember that two people

generally avoid sharing a two-seater sofa. They will tuck themselves happily at each end of a three-seater, though, whereas three occupants would find this arrangement cramped and uncomfortable.

If you're after a sofa in a particular width (to fit in a restricted space maybe, or to ensure comfortable use), either find a specialist supplier who makes them to order, or shop around until you find a suitable stock size. Bear in mind that dimensions vary widely not only from manufacturer to manufacturer, but also between the various ranges produced by each one. Increasingly, sofas are being made with a hinged construction that allows them to come apart for transporting and delivery. If you're worried about access, this option is worth investigating. Or look for unit (modular) ranges, which consist of single and corner units sold separately so that you can create whatever straight or angled seating arrangements you like. As your budget and space expand, you just add more units.

If possible, supplement your main seating with one or two fully upholstered chairs (there's no need for them to match

perfectly – each other or the sofa) or even those with padding on the seat and back only, which will provide your guests with at least some degree of comfort. Alternatively, express your individuality by buying (or even commissioning) a limited edition or one-off chair that is almost a work of art. If your dining table is in the same room, choose chairs that can double up as occasional seating, such as classic cane or bentwood chairs with seat pads and arms. One furnishing item that always comes in handy is a flat, padded footstool or ottoman, perhaps with a lift-up lid, that provides an extra surface and a useful storage compartment, as well as

Left above & left below: Modern technology is capable of producing occasional chairs in sinuous organic shapes that are more like 3D works of art than household furnishings.

Below: This appealingly chunky sofa provides a cosy sanctuary from even the most stressful life. Note the high back and arms, which offer maximum support whatever position you assume.

additional seating. At very least, make sure there are several thick cushions scattered around so that when you're faced with more visitors than seats, you can always sit comfortably on the floor.

covers & fabrics

Essentially, all upholstered seating has covers that are either stretched and tacked in place (known as 'fitted covers'), or cut and sewn separately, then slipped into position and fastened with zips, ties or Velcro (known as 'loose covers' or 'slipcovers'). Fitted covers give a finished, formal look. They are usually cheaper than loose ones (since less fabric is used and less work is involved), and they cannot be removed for cleaning. Although they cost more initially, loose covers are easy to remove for cleaning or simply when you want a change: perhaps from a dark, cosy winter fabric to a crisp, bright summer one. If you're considering a sofa with loose covers, find out how much a spare set will cost; some retailers even offer them periodically as a sales incentive.

Upholstered furniture usually swallows up a great deal of your decorating budget, so make sure that any covering materials you choose are suitable for their purpose. Fitted covers are constantly under tension, which makes them more vulnerable to wear than loose ones, so they require an extra-durable fabric. In most furnishing fabric departments, each roll is labelled according to its suitability: some fabrics are recommended for use as curtains only, some for curtains and loose covers, and others for curtains, loose and fitted covers. If you have any doubts, ask before you buy.

SOFA BEDS

A neat, stylish sofa bed can be ideal for accommodating occasional overnight guests. From the huge range available, choose one that unfolds from the seat, pulls out in a drawer or appears magically when you flatten the back and/or arms. The sofa-bed option is only worth exploring, though, if you can afford a solid, well-made model. Cheap sofa beds make neither comfortable beds (this may not matter if your house guests are infrequent) nor satisfactory sofas (this will matter if you expect the item in question to provide your main form of seating).

If putting friends up overnight is going to figure large in your domestic arrangements, consider supplementing your sofa with a simple studio or day bed or even a single divan, which you can dress up with a jazzy throw and a pile of cushions.

Certainly, if you're looking for something to sleep on every night in a studio flat, a good-quality mattress and base (see pages 179–83) is a much better choice than a sofa bed, which will give you considerably less support than the real thing. What's more, assembling or unfolding the mechanism every evening before you turn in will very quickly become an irritating chore.

TABLES, SHELVES & STORAGE FURNITURE

One of the main characteristics that sets apart cool, chic and well-planned living rooms from those that feel overly cluttered, inconvenient and inadequate, is the provision of appropriate storage facilities and a range of suitable surfaces for writing, displaying treasures and depositing all the detritus of everyday life.

tables

One of your most pressing needs will be for low surfaces positioned near the main seating area to hold permanent accessories such as lamps, and transitory clutter in the form of cups and plates, remote control handsets and reading

matter. Try to find side or coffee tables with shelves or drawers underneath, or use small, metal trunks, wooden blanket boxes or flat-topped wicker chests instead, and gain extra room inside. Adapting traditional storage furniture in this way can be a particularly useful trick, since coffee tables are a twentieth-century invention and it's sometimes hard to work them unobtrusively into a period scheme.

Contemporary designers, however, have made up for lost time, turning out hundreds of low-level occasional tables in every conceivable shape and material, from cane and pale hardwood to glass, metal and moulded plastic in delightfully juicy colours. If your living room is tiny, consider sets of neat, nesting tables or small, wooden ones that can be folded away flat when not in use.

When your dining area is in the living room, the table can double up for use as a writing and general-purpose work surface. (See if you can find one with a drawer to hold stationery and paperwork.) If your meals are to be served elsewhere, try to squeeze in a surface of similar proportions

(or perhaps a little smaller) to serve as a desk and hold items such as a chunky lamp and a drinks tray as well. Alternatively, shop laterally and look for something resembling a traditional console table (high but shallow, perhaps with a useful shelf underneath) among the kitchen furniture or even with the potting benches in the gardening department of a large home-furnishing store. A slimmed-down surface such as this works well against the wall or, if your sofa occupies a central position in the room, behind it.

Opposite: Traditional designs can combine style and function in clever ways. Here, a classic butler's tray folds away after use (above), while a scalloped-edge coffee table incorporates useful drawers (below).

This page: For maximum flexibility, choose tables on castors so you can move them around. The range shown above includes drawer units as well as a plain low table. At the left is a roomy horizontal storage grid with toughened glass top.

shelves

A sturdy and stylish run of shelves is a basic feature in almost every living room. The essential choice here is between freestanding shelves and built-in ones. Although they tend to be more expensive and less tailored to specific needs, freestanding shelves have the advantage of portability. You can move them freely around the room (or from room to room) and take them with you when you move. As they don't require a wall for support, they are more flexible in terms of positioning, so they can be placed in the middle of the room, perhaps acting as a divider (tall or short) between two activity areas.

One popular system that is even more adaptable is modular or cube shelving made from plastic, timber or man-made board such as MDF (medium-density fibreboard). Some modular ranges include drawer or door units that allow you to build a more comprehensive system. Another advantage is that you can start off with just one or two units and add more gradually.

Built-in shelves use space effectively: they can be custom-designed to suit your needs and require a smaller initial investment than shop-bought ones. If they're shoddily constructed, though, they will lower the tone of the room considerably. To avoid a saggy, student-ish look, avoid lightweight, adjustable systems. Instead, choose sturdy board for your shelves and give them plenty of strong support. Books, in particular, are very heavy indeed. To accommodate items ranging widely in height, vary the distance between your shelves (have the biggest gap at the bottom), or space them evenly for a tidier, more uniform effect. For the ultimate in ordered geometry, install a giant shelving grid in which each identical compartment has a separate visual personality.

When your shelves will be used just as much for storage as display, make life easier by providing some sort of camouflage for the least lovely items involved, such as a collection of videos or piles of back issues of your favourite magazines. If there aren't too many of these, store them all in smart containers, such as baskets, covered boxes (leather ones add a very upmarket touch) or small, metal chests, which will sit on (or beneath) your shelves

and look immaculate at all times. When the problem is even greater, fit a plain fabric, cane or wooden blind at ceiling level that will pull down to conceal one whole section of shelving completely.

To achieve a professional finish, fix a deep strip of plain timber or decorative moulding along the edge of each shelf. Finally, unfinished shelves, whether they're built-in or freestanding, have a sleeker, more fitted look when you paint them to match the walls.

Above: Consisting of nothing more than a sophisticated, scaled-up pegboard system, this ingenious storage wall accommodates shelves, CD racks, filing trays and even a wall light in an infinitely adjustable arrangement.

Right: Here, a freestanding shelf unit offers even more flexibility than usual: its hinged construction allows it to be extended in width or pivoted, as shown, to fit in a corner or act as a right-angled room divider.

Opposite: Part shelving system, part wall sculpture, this functional spiral allows the eye-catching graphics that adorn its contents to become an integral part of the display.

storage furniture

Your storage needs in the living room will be defined as clearly by your decorating foibles as the number of possessions you have. If you're happy for the television, VCR and sound system to be part of the furnishings, they can live on a shelf, a purpose-designed unit or a small table. But if you would prefer them to be hidden discreetly away, store them behind the doors of an inexpensive wardrobe or cupboard unit (drill holes in the back or the bottom for the wiring). Alternatively, keep the television and VCR on a low-level shelf beneath a small dining-height table, then drape it with a floor-length cloth that can be lifted up when you're ready for an evening's viewing. A wheeled trolley, too, will hold both these items and this can be tucked away surreptitiously when they're finished with.

Provide some form of roomy and easily accessible storage to hold items such as video tapes, audio cassettes, listings magazines and similar paraphernalia of the media age, as well as ordinary newspapers and magazines. It takes only a few of these things scattered around to throw even the tidiest

room into appalling disarray. Consider acquiring a lidded container of some kind, a wide, deep, open basket (originally intended to hold logs or laundry), or a family-sized chest of drawers for extra storage. When you come through the door half an hour before your dinner guests arrive, you can toss all the clutter inside to create an immediate impression of order and tranquillity. Those who have plenty of available floor space should look for a designer's plans chest, which will provide a generous surface area as well as huge, shallow drawers that can swallow up vast amounts of accumulated bits and pieces. Plans chests come in several heights: the smallest make capacious coffee tables, while the largest are more like outsize chests of drawers.

Make full use of all your available wall space by investing in a stylish wall-mounted CD rack to turn your Abba collection into a piece of sculptural installation art. In the

Left: Provide roomy storage baskets for the newspapers and magazines that threaten to engulf your space.

1 In times past, owners of fine libraries fixed lengths of fringe along the edge of all their shelves so that each volume was automatically dusted every time it was removed. Copy this idea to improve your housekeeping and add an unexpected touch of colour and movement.

2 Fix a cleaned-up railway sleeper in a prominent position as a massive, textural surface on which to arrange an informal and constantly changing display of drawings, prints, photographs and postcards.

3 A collection of books can contribute significantly to an atmosphere of cultural diversity and visual richness, but only when the volumes in question are genuinely part of your life and interests. Don't try for an instant library by buying a job lot from the charity shop or create achingly coordinated dust jackets for books you never open so they'll tone perfectly with your colour scheme. And, worst of all, avoid cutting off the spines to use as embellishment elsewhere. Instead, aim to find ways to explore the decorative potential of your real passions.

same vein, you can also fix a tiered magazine rack near the sofa to store all your favourite periodicals in the manner of newspapers in a brasserie.

If you don't have a spare surface for a well-stocked drinks tray, or sufficient cupboard space, keep your bottles in a deep, straight-sided basket that can sit on the floor, out of the way. Finally, if you yearn for a really vast surface on which to rest your beer cans and your feet, cut down the legs of a cheap softwood kitchen or dining table purchased from a mass-market chain or unearthed in a junk shop for an instant, inexpensive coffee table.

Above left: The intrusive modernity of your television and VCR will disappear completely when placed inside a purpose-made cabinet. This one has a subtly oriental look and a deep drawer that holds accessories, instruction manuals and video tapes.

Above: Storage furniture chosen for its self-effacing lines as well as its specific dimensions suits the nooks and crannies of a Victorian house perfectly.

lighting

In an area as multifunctional as the living room, your aim should be to create both soothing general lighting and appropriate illumination for specific tasks or activities. When you're formulating plans, remember that dark shades absorb more light than pale ones, so the deeper your colour scheme, the more light you'll need.

If the room already has fixed fittings, like wall or ceiling lights or recessed spots (and you have no objection to their positioning), replace any fussy or old-fashioned models with simple spots or uplighters. A dimmer switch connected to one, or several, of these easily will justify its cost by extending significantly the range of different moods and effects you can create.

When you're starting from scratch, particularly if you're still finding your way in terms of style, it's important to keep your lighting as flexible as possible. Instead of spending money on having new wiring chased into the walls and ceiling, invest in portable fittings like table, floor, clip-on and even novelty lamps. This way, you can move things around frequently and experiment with different effects. If you make a mistake or your tastes change and you want to try something new, the resulting cost and inconvenience will be minimal.

TOP TIPS

1 Before you settle on the final positions for your light fittings, check to make sure that illuminated bulbs will not be reflected in the television screen.
2 Never watch television in a darkened room. The harsh contrast between the bright screen and the area around it will cause eyestrain and headaches.
3 If your walls are bumpy and uneven, position lamps well away from them. Direct light will highlight every tiny imperfection.
4 To make a theatrical feature of a large plant, such as a bold cactus or a leafy palm or weeping fig, throw it into strong shadow using a small uplighter tucked surreptitiously behind the pot.

In many cases, a single fitting can serve more than one function: a well-chosen table lamp, for example, with a pale shade and a bulb of at least 60 watts, would be a perfectly adequate task lamp on a writing desk. In the same way, an uplighter or a clip-on spot focussed on a sculptural CD rack could act not only as ambient and informal accent lighting, but also as an important form of task illumination that allows you to locate a favourite disk or track without disturbing the dim and relaxed tranquillity of the room.

Choose at least one adjustable lamp with a beam that you can point in several directions according to what's going on in the room at the time. Or think about a standard (floor) lamp: just creeping back into fashion after years of undeserved neglect (and therefore increasingly widely available), these produce soft background illumination without taking up any valuable table or shelf space. In addition, when they are directed from above and behind a comfortable chair, the light they provide can be perfectly angled for shadowless reading.

Above left: This modest table lamp with its 1950s-inspired base produces gentle ambient lighting. Its narrow shade, however, makes it unsuitable for any bulb that is strong enough to read by.

Opposite: The dramatic silver-shaded standard lamps that dominate the guest quarters in this modern Mediterranean villa are by William Brandt.

WORKING AT HOME

One of the most significant social changes to accompany the new millennium is the huge increase in the number of people who work from home, either full or part time. The communications technology that has made this possible has revolutionized all our lives within the space of a single generation and will continue to do so as the relevant machinery and software become simultaneously more powerful, compact and affordable.

In order to serve the resulting demand for appropriately designed and scaled furniture, equipment and supplies, a whole new retail sector has grown up: the SOHO market (small office, home office). As a result, working from home can represent not only a blissful escape from the commuter nightmare and the corporate jungle; it can also allow you to spend your working life in a comfortable, calm and efficient environment that allows you to devote all your energy and resourcefulness to the job at hand.

choosing your spot

Even the most modestly proportioned living quarters are likely to afford some degree of choice in the location of a home work space. Few of us have the luxury of a separate room to work in, but if any juggling of functions or priorities would make this possible, then it's worth a try. In addition to acquiring extra space for your office, you would also gain the huge psychological advantage of being able to close the door on your professional life at the end of the working day.

After a dedicated home office, the next best option is to share quarters with a room used only part time. This could be a dining room in which a large table does double duty as a desk, or a guest bedroom, where a simple divan could be tucked into a corner and disguised with a tailored cover.

The vast majority of home workers, however, particularly those who are just starting out, set up shop in a corner or section of an existing room, usually the living room or

bedroom. It may be that the location of your work station is predetermined by the space available, but if you have a real choice, try to make your plans on a slightly broader basis. If the bedroom seems to be a more logical working area, consider whether you will mind spending two-thirds of your life enclosed inside the same four walls. If you work long, stressful hours, will your sleep be affected by the proximity of your business environment – a constant reminder of the work you still have to do? Other factors to take into account are the aesthetics of your location, noise pollution, available light and whether working at the front of your house or flat would involve placing valuable computer equipment in full view of passing traffic.

Above: Instead of a permanent work space, many people prefer what's known as a 'floating' office. Essentially, this involves a laptop computer and whichever surface is most appealing or available at any given time.

Opposite: This style-conscious studio occupant has chosen a storage tower whose seemingly precarious form is integral to its design. Note the adjustable chair and space-saving task light clamped to the desk.

furniture
& equipment

Every viable work space is comprised of a surface or desk, a chair, adequate lighting and whatever type and amount of storage space is required.

Work surfaces can be either built-in or freestanding. Like all built-in furnishings, the former make good use of space and can be adapted to whatever height is most comfortable for you. Freestanding desks are much more flexible in terms of positioning and come in a wide range of styles, both as purpose-designed models and kitchen or dining tables adapted for this use. The most recent addition to the range of available options is the specialized computer unit that includes not only a height-adjustable work surface, but also an integral cabling channel, dedicated shelving for items such as the CPU (central processing unit), printer and scanner, and storage compartments to hold things like floppy and zip disks and collections of CDs.

While almost any sturdy surface can be adapted for use as a desk, the chair you intend to sit on all day must be designed for this purpose. An old dining or occasional chair with a cushion placed on the seat will not do. What's

Above: This industrial-sized desk is supported by a suitably capacious storage pedestal designed to hold plans and drawings rather than hanging files; these live in a conventional cabinet on the left. Note the quirky L-shaped bookshelves that make the best possible use of an exceptionally narrow alcove.

Left: With a few design tweaks, the humble trolley becomes a perfect work station. Here, the top shelf is fixed at the right height for the screen, the pull-out drawer is intended for the keyboard and the bottom shelf is wide enough to support the printer at one end, then narrows toward the middle to become a foot rest.

Left: This sleek, built-in desk spans an
entire wall to provide a vast work surface
that takes up surprisingly little visual space.
Above it is a run of open storage boxes
that accommodate ring binders and box
files in a suitably neat and ordered fashion.

more, this kind of inadequate, but extremely common improvisation is likely to produce a wide range of health problems from constant tiredness to chronic headaches and strain in your back, neck and shoulders. Proper work or task chairs are evenly padded over the whole surface, with a seat that can be adjusted in height and a back that tilts to whatever angle best supports your vulnerable lower back area. To be completely stable, they should have five legs radiating out from a central pedestal. Castors fitted beneath will allow you to move freely around your work space. New task chairs can be prohibitively costly, but used ones in excellent condition (often set aside when big companies change their colour schemes) are widely available from second-hand office furniture outlets.

Almost as important as your chair is the provision you make for lighting your work space. Here, an adjustable task lamp that takes a bulb of at least 60 watts is the minimum requirement. To avoid working in your own shadow, position it on or above the side of your work surface opposite your dominant hand. If you're right-handed, position your desk light on the left. It's important, too, that you avoid glare of any kind, so back up this fitting with enough ambient illumination to soften the night-time contrast between your screen or work surface and a dimly lit room. During the day, natural daylight will fulfil the same function. To make sure the sun doesn't cause distracting reflections on your computer screen, though, try to position your desk at right angles to any window in close proximity.

organize your storage

One of the keys to maintaining a calm and orderly work space is to provide enough storage space to house everything you need within easy reach. Of course this will be easier if you begin by weeding out anything you don't use every day (old files, perhaps, back-up supplies of stationery or seldom-consulted reference books), which could be

shifted to a less-accessible cupboard or shelf. If your main storage area is a run of open shelves, invest in a range of colourful and stylish ring binders, box files or lidded containers that look smarter and less corporate than standard-issue grey or black ones. If you generate enough paperwork, look for a filing cabinet in whatever configuration of drawers is most suitable for your needs. These are available in plain or brightly painted metal, natural wood or wood veneer. Alternatively, buy an old battered one that's still serviceable and customize it with a fresh coat of paint in your chosen hue. Another extremely useful storage item is a wheeled trolley, which will hold a surprising amount of equipment and supplies, and will also roll neatly out of sight when it's no longer needed.

setting up
your work station

Particularly if you sit at a desk and screen for long hours, the ergonomics of your work space – that is, the way you relate to the furniture, equipment and space around you – will have a profound effect on your general well-being as well as your productivity. The recommended height for a desk is about 63–76 cm (25–30 in), with a keyboard positioned about 5–6 cm (2–2½ in) lower. Here, the vital question is whether you can sit up straight while you work, without hunching your back or rounding your shoulders. If you are taller or shorter than average, adjust the seat of your chair until you feel comfortable. To minimize the stress on your forearms and wrists that can contribute to the misery of RSI (repetitive strain injury), make sure they run parallel to the floor in a single, straight line: many people find a pull-out keyboard tray and/or a wrist rest helpful.

Your thighs, too, should be parallel with the floor and should clear the underside of the desk with plenty of room to spare. A foot rest, whether it's a smart, purpose-made one, a traditional padded stool or an old, wooden box you've pressed into service, will make a dramatic difference to your comfort. To avoid strain on your neck, position your computer screen about 46–61 cm (18 x 24 in) away from your eyes and slightly below them. Those whose job involves a lot of keying in should avoid working from originals laid flat on the adjacent surface. Instead, buy a document holder to support papers vertically beside the screen.

Right: An ergonomically healthy work station is the single most important element in any office.

Opposite: In this cool, clean-edged work corner, the whole repertoire of small-space decorating tricks has been deployed. First, an all-over colour treatment – on the walls, window, pipes, woodwork, radiator, shelves and furniture – reduces visual clutter dramatically. Transparent storage boxes (on the shelf and the desk) seem to recede into the background, while huge metal ones on castors can be wheeled away in seconds. Finally, the chocolatey brown colour of the floor is carried over the skirting board to make the room look considerably larger.

5

Modern kitchens have a heavy cultural burden to bear: as well as their multifarious practical functions, they need to reflect current

kitchens

design trends, contain a prescribed selection of gadgets and appliances, and fulfil a dual role as drop-dead status symbol and 'heart of the home'. Achieving all this in one room is impossible. Instead, create a space full of colours and objects you love, where you can perform tasks efficiently, conveniently, safely and, above all, pleasurably.

PLANNING

To some extent, the demands you make on your kitchen will vary according to how large a role cooking and entertaining play in your life. People for whom food is a controlling passion will clearly have a much wider and more complex design agenda than those who want only to prepare simple meals, snacks and drinks.

At a fairly early stage, you'll have to decide which major appliances you want to fit in and how large or complex you'd like these to be (see pages 148–51). As always, think through each option carefully: if you live alone and have little interest in cooking, for example, you may consider a dishwasher to be completely unnecessary. In fact, a small model might be a very wise investment since it would swallow up dirty cups, plates and glasses as you use them. Then, if you turn the

Below: With its powerful extractor hood, catering-sized sink and appliances, and extensive batterie de cuisine, this kitchen is equipped for serious cooking. Note the practical, yet stylish, wire shelf with hanging rail fitted directly underneath.

Single-line kitchens provide a workable small-space option. In this example, the fridge should go on the far right, away from the heat of the cooker.

Galley kitchens are also limited in size, but they contain plenty of work space. Create a neat work triangle by placing the fridge opposite the sink.

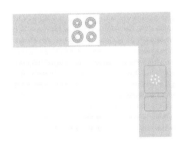

L-shaped layouts suit bigger, squarer kitchens. Here, the fridge works best on the far left, where it clears the cooker yet allows an unbroken run of worktop.

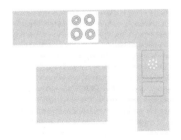

Island units offer maximum flexibility. Tuck a separate fridge and freezer under the counter, or put the sink there and a full-sized fridge/freezer on the right.

machine on only when it's full, you'll keep your kitchen free of clutter, save time and effort, and conserve energy as well. (Buy extra everyday glass and crockery if you don't have enough.) With small appliances too, it's not only foodies who benefit; someone who never looks at a recipe but loves fruity milkshakes, cocktails and freshly ground coffee might get just as much use from a liquidizer as the most enthusiastic amateur chef. Think, too, about whether you want to leave room in your plan for one or two items that you can't afford to purchase right now, but hope to acquire within the next few years.

The other major variable is the number of tasks, apart from food preparation, that have to be accommodated here. Although the kitchen is the most popular spot for the washing machine, for example, think about whether it could go somewhere else. Locating it in the bathroom, for example, or in a cupboard nearby perhaps, might do much more than free up valuable kitchen space; if you dry your clothes over the bath and keep your laundry basket nearby, this arrangement would save you a great many steps as well.

starting from scratch

The cheapest, and by far the most popular type of kitchen is a fitted one, put together from a number of standard units chosen to make the best possible use of space and provide whatever accessories and storage facilities (drawers, cupboards, etc.) are required. Chosen and installed with skill and flair, a built-in kitchen can also add considerably to the value of your home.

Over the last few years, enthusiasm has also been growing for the non-fitted kitchen, in which most of the elements are separate and freestanding: a chest of drawers, maybe, a table, a cupboard, a shelf unit, and a work bench that houses the sink and draining board. While purists insist on discovering and combining these elements themselves, several manufacturers now produce whole ranges of freestanding kitchen furniture from which clients can choose the pieces they want. Non-fitted kitchens have a less clinical look than built-in ones and they make it easier to accommodate surfaces of different heights and materials. Like all freestanding furnishings, they can be shifted around, added to and even taken with you to your next home.

In terms of what goes where, shops and showrooms who specialize in kitchens usually offer a free planning service. When you're still at the browsing stage though, always take with you a floor plan marked with accurate measurements and the position of doors, windows, radiators, plumbing, sockets, etc. so you have some basis for initial discussions. The plan you end up with should revolve around a basic work triangle formed by the sink, the hob and the fridge. These should be positioned as closely together as possible, with the sink and hob on the same (or adjoining) sides so that you never have to carry saucepans of boiling water across the floor to drain vegetables or pasta. Make sure, too, that

lighting

While kitchens do not require the same degree of lighting flexibility as more multifunctional areas, they do rely heavily on clear, strong illumination. This is not only important for reading recipes and preparing food, but also for reasons of cleanliness and safety. When you're drawing up your initial floor plan, try to make sure that the main work surface enjoys the full benefit of any natural light by placing it either under (or adjacent to) a window rather than on the opposite wall. At night, a central fitting (pendant, fluorescent strip or recessed downlighter) is unlikely to be enough, so supplement this with task illumination of at least 100 watts positioned to cast shadow-free light onto the work surface, hob and sink: or in the form of under-shelf strips or tubes, perhaps, clip-on spots, or downlighters fitted beneath wall-hung cupboards.

At the same time, you'll appreciate the option of a small, warm, friendly light for times when you don't want total darkness but full task illumination is too bright. This is particularly important if you sometimes eat in the kitchen. If one of your existing fittings can't be used in this way, try to find room for a small table or clip-on lamp, or a pendant suspended low over the table or at one end of the work surface. Or opt for candlelight, on its own or used with one of the above.

the fridge (or a separate freezer) is not next to any source of direct heat such as a radiator, an oven and tumble dryer.

Try to fit in plenty of worktop around your triangle and anywhere else where there is room; you can never have too much. And if there isn't enough space in your kitchen for a full-sized table, maybe you could squeeze in a small flap-down surface that folds up flat against the wall when it is not being used.

revamping
what's there

When you inherit a kitchen that's perfectly functional, if not aesthetically inspiring, there's a great deal that you can do to stamp it with your own personality. If the carcass is solid, replace the worktop and doors with new ones; most tops and doors are made to a standard size so you should have no problem finding something you like. Or give the existing doors a completely new look by covering them with sheets of laminate, thin ply or metal (stainless steel or zinc), or simply paint them and add different handles. For wooden or MDF units, use eggshell or gloss paint in the normal way; laminate surfaces require a little more preparation and a special paint formulated to do this job; many of these come as a two-part system (primer and topcoat). Finally, if the existing units are too low, buy a chunky butcher's-block chopping board to raise the main work area up to a comfortable working height.

walls, floors
& windows

In the kitchen, as many surfaces as possible should be at least wipeable, so choose silk rather than matt-finish paint. Many companies now produce special bathroom and kitchen ranges, which are designed to be especially resistant to condensation and easy to clean.

Floors must, of course, be non-slip and fully washable. A lot of spilled water or a washing machine that leaks can damage or warp a solid wooden floor or give it a slick surface, so vinyl, laminate or linoleum might be a better choice. Very hard surfaces – tiles, slate, brick, etc. – are perfectly practical and exceptionally hard-wearing but they feel cold underfoot, they show no mercy to any item of china or glass that gets dropped on them, and are extremely tiring to stand on for long periods. (If your preferred surface is especially heavy, check that the floor will bear the weight before you buy.)

Textiles attract grease and cooking smells, so choose blinds instead of curtains for your windows or submit to the charm of fresh cotton and come to grips with washing and ironing it regularly. If you do decide on curtains for the kitchen, it's vital that you guard against accidental fires by keeping them well away from the hob, or any other heat-producing appliance.

colouring your kitchen

The only colours that really don't work in a kitchen are very dark shades, which both absorb light and disguise dirt. If you long for a particularly bright or quirky shade, however, such as golden yellow, salmon pink or cool aqua, this could be an ideal place to use it. In this room, particularly though, it's wise to keep your decorating scheme simple. Kitchens are full of colourful objects and eye-catching packaging anyway, and if there are different hues on the walls, ceiling and storage units as well, the overall effect is likely to be one of extreme visual clutter rather than stunning chromatic boldness.

Above: A fresh blue-and-white scheme encourages the vibrant hues of the fruit bowl, the larder and the china cupboard to become an integral part of the room.

Opposite: The satiny sheen of stainless steel dominates every surface in this streamlined kitchen, from the integral sink and work surface to the cantilevered shelving and the pots and pans on display.

STORAGE

Creating a successful storage system is not just about working out how much space you need; it also involves knowing what kind of storage will work best for you and your kitchen. Here, as always, the first step is to take stock of all your requirements.

assessing your needs

When it comes to food and general household products, one of the most important factors to consider is your shopping habits. Do you order basics frequently over the internet and regularly pop into a convenience store or supermarket after work to pick up anything else you need, or do you, like many busy people, organize one huge shopping trip every few weeks? If you tend toward the latter arrangement, make sure you have somewhere to accommodate all your purchases, especially bulky items such as washing powder, kitchen rolls and bags of dried pasta. Infrequent trips to the recycling centre will also mean

growing piles of newspapers, bottles and cans, so give some thought to where these might go. Ideally they should be stored in a garage, shed or basement, but if that's not possible, a large basket to hold the papers and similar containers (or maybe large canvas bags suspended from coat hooks) for bottles and cans will look much neater than uncontrolled heaps on the floor, or in flimsy plastic carriers. You'll need at least one tall cupboard for awkward and often unsightly items such as the vacuum cleaner, ironing board and any mops or brooms you might use, and this is often a sensible place to store your recycling as well.

When there isn't enough storage space in a kitchen, most of the overspill tends to end up on the work surface. This is particularly true of small appliances and pieces of equipment, so if you have a weakness for technology, make sure you have somewhere to house it all. It's one thing to share your worktop with items in daily use, like a microwave oven, a kettle and a toaster, but it takes only a few more machines of a similar size (food processor, juicer, electric can opener or coffee maker, perhaps) to cover it almost completely. For the same reason, if you

Opposite: Put visually appealing and frequently used items on display (left), and tuck unlovely necessities neatly away in drawers (right).

Above: This unusual base unit has been made without doors so the contents are visible. Shelves fixed at different levels minimize wasted space.

can sense the beginnings of a serious cookbook collection, consider organizing a home for it elsewhere.

It's not difficult to work out exactly how much room you need for the things you already own, but the overwhelming likelihood is that you'll collect more of everything as time goes on. If possible, be generous with your storage allocation at the very beginning.

exploring
the options

Armed with at least a rough idea of your needs, you can start weighing up your choices. If you're having kitchen units installed and your budget is limited, save costs by choosing a range that comes in flatpack form. Unless you are skilled at DIY though, or have access to someone who is, it's worth

paying a professional to install them. Rigid, ready-assembled units cost more than flat-packs and are often available in a wider variety of sizes and finishes; kitchens sold in this way are also more likely to be available as part of an optional package that includes measuring up and fitting.

Once you've found a range you like, take a close look at all the units available so you can decide which ones you want: a stack of drawers, maybe, a pull-out saucepan rack, or a door-mounted rubbish bin. See if any of the cabinets come with adjustable shelving so that small items can be stored without leaving several inches of wasted space above them. If the shelves are fixed, look out for special fittings, often sold separately, that are designed to make the best of them. These include clip-on baskets, tiered racks, can tidies and tray organizers, which look like giant toast racks and hold bakeware, chopping boards and pan lids as well as trays. If you are left-handed, or you want to fit a cupboard in a restricted corner, check whether any units come with doors that can be hinged on either side. Some base units offer flexibility in terms of height as well – a valuable facility for those who are taller than average. In some cases, this is

Below: Use a workmanlike trolley to hold your drinks tray and glasses, or as a portable storage unit for china, saucepans or non-perishable foods in attractive bottles, jars and packets. Some models are available with adjustable shelves, useful hooks and locking castors.

to the cooker. (If you find yourself using the same one or two saucepans every day, save space and time by leaving them out on the hob permanently.)

On any remaining wall space, fit a wire storage grid, a traditional wooden or metal plate rack, a peg rail or simply a row of hooks, all of which are much less visually intrusive than solid cabinets. Another ingenious option is a ceiling-fixed hanging rack, which will hold a huge amount of equipment (saucepans, colanders, jugs, ladles, etc.) without taking up any work surface or wall area at all. Without cumbersome wall cabinets your room will look bigger and lighter, and the risk of banging your head on an open door is removed. (To achieve this effect without sacrificing cupboard space, replace the doors with simple roller or roll-up blinds, which conceal the contents without getting in the way.)

saving space

When the room you're trying to furnish is the tiniest of galley kitchens, it's sometimes impossible to fit standard units along both sides and yet still have enough room between them to manoeuvre comfortably. One useful trick is to choose base units only in the same way. Along one side, however – instead of the larger cabinets intended for this purpose – install those meant to be fixed above the worktop, which are only about half as deep. Of course this will mean that you have a standard work surface on one side and one of half-depth on the other.

If, despite your best efforts, you still can't fit everything in, then consider removing a few bulky bits of seldom-used equipment (roasting tin, large saucepans, serving platters, etc.) to a deep shelf fixed above the door. Alternatively, you could even move it all to another spot altogether, such as a box hidden under the bed or behind the sofa.

achieved by fixing units to the wall rather than resting them on the floor; other ranges have clip-on plinths that conceal individually adjustable legs (handy for uneven floors).

In a small kitchen (or 'if you just prefer a simpler look), consider installing base units only, which will hold all your cooking and cleaning equipment, small appliances and bulky tins, packets and jars. On the wall above, fix a row of long, sturdy shelves to accommodate all the visually appealing items you use regularly where they'll be within easy reach: everyday china and glass near the sink, supplies of tea and coffee next to the kettle, sharp knives in a safe holder beside the chopping board, and wooden spoons and utensils close

Right: To magick a significant amount of storage space out of thin air, install a ceiling-fixed hanging rack. The shape of your kitchen and the amount of equipment you possess will dictate your choice of shape and design. This jumbo version consists of a row of strong parallel rails, but a more compact round or square model – or even a single bar – may be a more suitable for a first home. To hold small, light items, consider a hanging grid made of timber strips or wire mesh.

Above: Ceramic sinks suggest the quaint charm of a farmhouse kitchen, but they are also easily chipped and a chipped sink is quite likely to harbour dirt, germs and bacteria.

Below: This sculptural chrome mixer tap has plenty of room underneath to accommodate tall jugs and vases, and large items like baking pans, roasting pans and oven racks.

SINKS & TAPS

A washing area that doesn't work, perhaps because the sink is too small, the surface chips or the taps are slippery, can be a major source of frustration. However, it's not a complicated or expensive process to get it right.

materials & finishes

Most kitchen sinks are made from stainless steel, enamelled pressed steel, composite or fireclay (ceramic material).

- **Stainless steel** is slightly misnamed since it will mark, but the marks can be removed. It has a durable finish and a simple, professional look that makes it a popular, practical choice. Stainless steel sinks are affordably priced.
- **Enamelled steel** sinks are usually white, with an appealingly basic quality; a few come in bright colours too. Hard knocks can chip the surface, but otherwise enamel compares with stainless steel in practicality and price.
- **Composite** sinks are made from a mix of stone particles and acrylic resin. They cost slightly more than stainless or enamelled steel and they come in a wide range of colours and finishes, some of which resemble stone or granite.
- **Ceramic** sinks are more expensive still, and the most popular (deep, white and rectangular) are coveted largely for their nostalgic charm; they chip quite easily.

In the luxury bracket are sinks made from brass (which look wonderful, but mark badly), teak (which has a rich finish and is kind to breakables), and cast iron (which is very heavy).

style & fitting

A dainty round or oval sink may seem a wise choice when you're trying to save space, but you'll soon change your mind if you can't submerge a baking tray or even a large platter in it. The most practical choice is rectangular and as large as possible. When space is no problem, a double sink is worthwhile since it allows you to do two things at the same time (soak dishes and rinse salad, for example). If that's not possible, one big sink is far better than two little ones,

and specialist ones such as brass, pewter and bronze becoming increasingly common.

Separate (or pillar) taps are less popular in the kitchen than mixer taps with a single, swivelling spout: for maximum manoeuvrability underneath, choose one that curves high over the sink. Mixer taps are operated either by different HOT and COLD handles or levers, or by a single lever, which lifts, angles or turns to control the pressure and temperature. Whatever design you eventually choose, make sure you can operate your taps easily, even with wet, soapy hands.

Most taps fit into holes in the sink, but some are plumbed through the surface and others into the wall behind. Popular in catering kitchens, wall-mounted taps leave worktops uncluttered and easy to clean. Some taps are available with an inbuilt water purification system, while others have a matching hand spray.

but a more workable compromise here may be what's known as one-and-a-half sinks: one full-sized version and one small, shallow one, which at least allows you to fill a jug or rinse an apple while the main sink is in use.

Sinks are fitted in one of three ways. Most are inset into the work surface, either alone or with one or two draining boards attached, and sealed around the edge to make them watertight. Some sinks are moulded in one integral piece with the draining board or boards and the work surface. Least common, and most difficult to install, are undermounted sinks, which are set directly beneath a precisely cut hole in the work surface. Undermounted sinks suit kitchens that include a dishwasher since, by definition, they never have an integral draining board and ensuring a waterproof seal is a tricky, specialist job.

Look for a sink that comes with a range of accessories: a colander, wire basket or chopping board that fits neatly into the opening will not only make the sink more useful, it also extends the size of your work surface. A draining rack can be used to store many more items (and hold them more securely) than you can pile up on the flat surface. The most affordable of these are made from wood or rubber-coated wire, while chrome and stainless steel versions are considerably more expensive.

choosing your taps

Whether your signature look is sleek and designer-like, strongly historical, or straightforwardly practical, you may be surprised by the sheer range of suitable style choices. Chrome is probably the most popular finish of all, with white and coloured versions following close behind

This page: Choose a mixer tap fitted with a single lever (top) or separate HOT and COLD handles (centre). Alternatively, some people prefer separate pillar taps (below).

WORK SURFACES & SPLASHBACKS

The food preparation area of your kitchen represents the front line when it comes to domestic practicality. More than any other surface, your worktop has to be durable, hygienic, waterproof and resistant to heat, stains and scratches. Whatever material you choose, make sure all the fitting is skilfully done so there are no gaps left to trap dirt and germs. Finally, don't expect miracles from it: use a separate chopping board for cutting and slicing, and place red-hot pans on a mat or trivet, never directly on your worktop.

worktop options

From the wide range of materials available, choose one that suits your style, your budget and the kind of wear you're likely to inflict:

- **Laminate** is the most popular choice for domestic work surfaces. Available in a huge variety of solid colours, patterns and wood or stone effects, it is sold in large sheets then cut to fit. Laminate comes in a wide range of qualities (and therefore prices): the cheapest warp, stain and scratch, though, so invest in a top-quality branded version such as Formica.
- **Stainless steel** has gained a much wider market in the last few years, but it's always been the surface of choice in professional kitchens. Although this is a very

fashionable material, the trend is unlikely to fade since stainless steel is almost indestructible, hygienic and totally waterproof. Stainless steel worktops are expensive, though, and require considerable upkeep but the faint scratches they develop with age add to their charm.

- **Solid hardwood**, such as iroko, teak, maple and sycamore, is warm, beautiful and practical, and it mellows with age. It requires high maintenance, though, even after it's sealed and seasoned, and it's expensive. Cheaper, quick-fix alternatives are laminated ply, sealed MDF and timber veneers.
- **Ceramic tiles** offer a wide choice in terms of colour and design and they can be matched to floors and splashbacks. Not all tiles are suitable, though; they have to be specially fired to make them tough enough for worktops (which also makes them pricey). Quarry tiles have a more durable surface than highly glazed ones, but all tiles tend to trap dirt in their grouting.
- **Marble** is a smooth and luxurious surface, but it is very expensive and prone to staining. If you enjoy making pastry, invest in a cool, non-stick marble board – inset into your worktop or free-standing – for rolling it out.
- **Granite** is as smooth and cool as marble, but much more durable, less porous and easier to clean. Granite work surfaces have a less formal look than those made from marble, but they are also very expensive.
- **Slate** costs less than other stone surfaces and has a rougher texture. It needs sealing and polishing, but ages well. Slate will scratch, but tiny marks can be sanded away.
- **Solid, synthetic surfaces**, sold under brand names such as Corian and Avonite, are acrylic or polyester based and resemble natural or coloured stone. They are chip-proof, non-porous, heat-resistant and seam-free, and some of them can be moulded with integral sinks

and drainers. This type of work surface is at the high
end of the price spectrum.

- **Poured concrete** can scream industrial chic or country
simplicity. Reinforced to make it durable and non-porous,
it can also be tinted or textured and is usually cast on site,
which makes it seamless and adaptable for worktops of
irregular size and/or shape. Concrete is very heavy and
falls into the medium price range.

splashbacks

The wall behind the worktop – the splashback – needs
protection, but the demands made on it are much less
heavy. For classic good looks, practicality and value, white
tiles will always win out; fix them in grid formation, or
stepped like bricks. Coloured or hand-painted tiles have
a different look and represent a more serious financial
outlay. To blend the splashback into the wall, fix tongue-
and-groove cladding then paint it to match; or if you
have a stainless steel work surface, create an unbroken
finish by using the same material for the splashback, but in
a thinner sheet to reduce costs.

Other ideas include varnished plywood (with/without a
coloured stain), toughened glass, corrugated plastic, rubber
flooring, roofing zinc and sheet aluminium or perspex.

Above left: Metal work surfaces
are very durable and easy to
clean, and their reflective
sparkle provides a perfect foil
for vivid colours and
contemporary shapes. Note the
matching handles and switches.

Above: Large sheets of clear
perspex protect the plain
painted wall behind this
hardwood work surface
without imposing any visual
distraction on the spare, natural
scheme in this kitchen.

MAJOR APPLIANCES

Every kitchen needs at least two largish domestic appliances: a fridge (with or without a freezer) to store fresh food at suitably low temperatures, and a cooker to heat it up. Many households, even single-person households, also have a washing machine or a washer/dryer (or even a separate tumble dryer) and more and more include a dishwasher too.

At one time, all these machines had very much the same look: they were white and shiny. Now, many come disguised as retro classics (particularly fridges and cookers), or in brightly coloured enamel or satiny stainless steel. Most manufacturers also make appliances designed to blend visually into the units ('built-in' models take a fascia that matches the cupboard doors, while 'fully integrated' ones are completely invisible), but these cost more than ordinary appliances and are often an extra expense that's difficult to justify.

As well as becoming increasingly stylish, modern domestic machines are far more energy efficient than their forebears; most are now labelled according to a grading system so you can see which are the most and least energy efficient. Making the right choices in this department will not only benefit the environment, it will also reduce your running costs.

food storage

Here, the most practical choice is likely to be some form of combination fridge/freezer. The overall size of the appliance will vary with your space and budget, but the relative size of each compartment depends more on your own habits and needs: how often you shop, how much frozen food you buy, and how much home-cooked food you freeze. Larger households often support a separate full-sized freezer as well as a fridge, but this is very unlikely to be necessary when there are just one or two of you. If you're prepared to pay for considerably increased flexibility, invest in one of the newer models fitted with an ingenious central convertible section that can alternate between fridge and freezer at the flick of a switch. Or, to allow an uninterrupted expanse of work surface, choose separate, under-counter appliances

cooking

Enthusiastic and knowledgeable cooks are more than likely to be familiar with the various types of cooker on the market, and may already have a strong idea of what they want: a separate oven and hob, perhaps, with all manner of specialized extras and accessories. If your interest in cooking is more functional, though, and you're unsure of what you need, stick to a simple conventional cooker, which is not only less intimidating but also less likely to go wrong.

One way to do this is by buying a re-conditioned model; those from the 1940s, 1950s and 1960s are becoming more and more sought after for their appealing lines and supreme operational simplicity. They are also cheaper than some of the flashy new designs and constitute very impressive recycling. At the other end of the market are the newly fashionable professional and semi-professional ranges that offer increased capacity, industrial styling and powerful heat (with price tags to match). These catering ranges may have additional features such as a barbecue, griddle plate or wok ring, but because they are intended for (or inspired by) professional kitchens, they tend to be free of twinky accessories such as pre-set timers, self-cleaning ovens and automatic controls.

Most domestic cookers are fuelled by either gas or electricity: gas is quicker to respond and easier to see, while electricity offers a range of more sophisticated extras such as fan ovens, which cook faster and at a lower temperature. Your choice of fuel may be dictated by what's available in your house or flat, but if you have access to both, consider a combination appliance with an electric oven and a gas hob, which offers the best of both worlds. Again, the range of sizes is enormous, but even if you don't intend to entertain very often, make sure the model you choose is big enough to cope with the few occasions when you will need it: cooking a family-sized turkey at Christmas perhaps, or heating through enough canapés for a drinks party.

ranged side by side. When you're deciding which size to buy, bear in mind too that a freezer works better when it's full to capacity, while a fridge is more efficient when the air inside can circulate freely. However you manage it, a four-star freezer (one that can freeze efficiently and not just store already-frozen food) is worthwhile for even the most dedicated non-cook, since it will provide a constant supply of basics such as fresh milk, bread, coffee and Parmesan cheese, as well as emergency ready-prepared meals.

Features you might like to look out for in a fridge or a fridge/freezer include: a super-fast freezing facility, extra-deep door shelving, door alarm, ice-making device and chilled drink dispenser. If your optimum floor plan requires the door to be hinged on the left, make sure this is possible, and if your floor is uneven, check for individually adjustable feet. Finally, whichever model you choose, take care of it by never putting warm food inside, and making sure to clean and defrost it regularly.

you were to do all your laundry by hand. (Machines also do a much better job, since they raise the water to a higher temperature than your hands could ever bear, even with rubber gloves on.)

DRYING

While it's not necessary (and arguably inadvisable) to tumble dry all your clothes, a dryer is extremely useful for handling large items such as sheets, and for things like towels and bathrobes, which have a much less scratchy feel to them when they're tumble-dried. If you have room for a separate dryer (some are specially designed to stack on top of the washing machine), it might be worth considering; they are not vastly expensive and they're also not too difficult to accommodate. There are two main types of dryer to choose from. Venting dryers, which duct the moist air directly outside through a wall or window, are the cheapest, but they're also somewhat limited in terms of location. The other type, which cost slightly more, are called condensing dryers because they cool and condense the moisture they remove. This can then run away down the drain, or collect in a reservoir, which must be emptied regularly. The greatest advantage with a reservoir, of course, is that the dryer doesn't have to be installed anywhere near a sink – it can live almost anywhere within reach of a power outlet.

laundry

No matter how cool and trendy your local launderette has become, it can never match the convenience of washing your clothes in individual loads when it suits you (or when they're dirty), instead of having to plan one huge weekly session into your schedule. The relevant appliances here are a conventional washing machine, a tumble dryer and a combined washer/dryer.

WASHING

Washing machines don't vary as much in size and capacity as fridges and cookers, although there are several slimline ones available. Their price is determined more by the number of features offered, and the general quality and reliability of the brand. Some of the options you should look for are: an economy or low-temperature setting, a handwash/wool/delicates cycle, a half-load facility, an extra-rinse cycle (useful for those with sensitive skin) and a variable spin speed. The key here is to take advantage of the programmes that suit you without paying for several dozen more you'll never touch.

Most impressive of all is 'fuzzy logic' or self monitoring, which enables the machine to sense the size and condition of the load and adjust the water and detergent accordingly. Across the board, of course, modern machines use much less water than earlier ones and dramatically less than you would use if

The main drawback with combined washer/dryers is that they can only dry half the wash load at one time; they are also much slower than commercial tumble dryers. For a small household, however, this is not likely to be a problem, and the advantages of being able to produce clean, dry bed and bath linen without heaving it to the launderette or draping it around your rooms is considerable. One feature to look for is a high spin speed, which reduces drying time.

If you can't manage any kind of electric drying facility, explore the possibility of an old-fashioned clothes airer on a pulley system that lifts it up to ceiling height, perhaps in the kitchen or even a lofty hall. This will at least give you somewhere to hang your laundry where it's not in your way.

IRONING

Almost all domestic irons now provide steam and cold-water spray as well as variable heat, and some even clean and descale themselves too. The question of weight is a personal one: some people like a light iron while others find a heavy one easier to use, but performance is much more dependent on temperature, steam and the easy movement of the soleplate. Look for one made of stainless steel or coated with a special non-stick finish.

dishwashing

It could be argued that a dishwasher is especially useful in a one- or two-person household when only a few items are used at a time (see page 136). Also, like washing machines, dishwashers are much more efficient than their manual equivalent. However, some fine tableware and cutlery is not suitable for machine washing, so establish this before you buy anything new, and stick to handwashing valuable heirloom plates, bone-handled cutlery, hand-painted china and any items that are made of wood.

Most dishwashers offer a choice of programmes, depending on the size of load and how soiled it is; whether it contains dishes encrusted with burnt-on food or teacups and plates only. (Some machines can actually work this out for themselves with the same 'fuzzy logic' used by washing machines.) Each programme consists of cycles that wash, rinse and dry the dishes, and you will need to keep your machine supplied with water-softening salt and liquid rinse aid as well as special detergent.

When it come to size, dishwashers tend to be described by the number of place settings they hold: standard machines take twelve, slimline machines six to nine, and compact machines (those that sit on the worktop) four to five. When you're thinking about possible locations, remember that dishwashers require proximity to the cold water supply, the waste pipe and a power outlet. If you're intending to use your machine at night, find out just how much noise it makes before you commit yourself.

Opposite: Most traditional clothes airers (top) come with end pieces and pulley only, leaving you to supply timber battens in your chosen length. Large appliances have come a long way since the days when they were known as 'white goods'. This funky tumble dryer (below) comes in several other circus-bright colours.

Left: This slimline dishwasher takes eight place settings, which is more than enough to suit a small household.

SMALL APPLIANCES

Once regarded as being among the most boring items any of us ever acquired, small kitchen appliances are now not only complex and sophisticated; some of them have also become contemporary style icons. Even if you can't afford any of these designer objects of desire, however, try to find appliances with simple lines and straightforward styling.

The single appliance most of us would find it hardest to live without is an electric kettle. For some people, a microwave is just as vital, while for others a machine that produces perfect toast tops the list.

kettles

Don't even consider buying a kettle that isn't electric; apart from being much slower, they also use considerably more energy to do the same job. (When you want to steam vegetables or poach eggs, never wait for water to boil in a saucepan. Boil it in the kettle, then transfer it to the pan.)

The basic choice here is between a traditional, squat kettle, which is likely to be made of metal (either chrome, stainless steel or enamelled), or a jug kettle (tallish, cylindrical and probably plastic – sometimes in a range of delicious, translucent jelly colours). For small households, a jug kettle is best since these can boil up a mugful of water more quickly than their broadly based alternatives. Most contemporary kettles have a water gauge, automatic switch-off and cordless technology, while some appealing optional extras include automatic descaling, programmable temperature control and a super-fast heating element.

microwave ovens

Old-fashioned microwaves had many limitations: they were excellent for thawing food, heating meals and drinks in minutes, cooking vegetables and baking potatoes very quickly, but hopeless for anything that involved crispness or browning. The latest generation, however, can cook by grilling and convection too, in the same way as a normal oven, and so they are much more useful. To make life even easier, look for a model that doesn't require you to judge the cooking time: just indicate on the panel the type of food or liquid you're putting in and close the door. The machine weighs the item and does the sums so all you have to do is press the start button and wait.

Remember that you can't put dishes or lids made of metal or paper into a microwave, and anything sealed, such as a sausage, has to be pricked first so the steam can escape during cooking. If in doubt, always follow the manufacturer's recommendations.

toasters

Here, style choices vary from industrial chic in chrome or stainless steel to funky, coloured plastic. Most toasters accommodate two or four slices of bread, but some have a special sandwich toaster or bun-warmer facility included as well. Other useful features to look out for are a defrost mode, thick-and-thin slice adjuster, cancel button and a wide range of temperature settings.

food mixers & processors

The serious players here are: hand whisks, food mixers, food processors and blenders.

- **Hand whisks** are small, light and easy to use, making them ideal for soups, drinks, eggs and sauces.
- **Food mixers** are best for cakes, batters and whisking egg

whites, and perfect for making creamy mashed potatoes. A hand mixer will do these jobs just as well as a bulky countertop one with a stand and bowl. Some take attachments for chopping, slicing, etc., but they don't perform these tasks as efficiently as a food processor.

- **Food processors** are brilliant for chopping, slicing, mincing, puréeing and grating. Some will mix and whisk too, but not as well as a food mixer.
- **Blenders (or liquidizers)** make milkshakes, soups, sauces, purées, cocktails and juices (for which you have to add water). A small attachment is often included for grinding nuts and coffee beans.

juicers

These machines differ from blenders in that they don't require any water to be added, so the resulting fruit or vegetable juice is concentrated. Make sure you look for a juicer that will take any suitable fruit or vegetable – some of them are just glorified citrus presses.

coffee makers

If you can't bear to open your eyes in the morning without drinking a powerful dose of caffeine, consider investing in a conventional filter coffee machine or one that makes real espresso and cappuccino.

other machines

According to your culinary and gastronomic quirks, you might also be tempted by one or several of the following: an electric wok, a deep fryer, a wine safe or a dedicated machine for making pasta, bread, popcorn, ice-cream or toasted sandwiches.

Opposite: A toaster with classic lines (above) will suit any style of kitchen. The stainless steel kettle (below) combines sleek detailing with a comforting, rather chubby shape.

This page: A traditional blender (above) makes perfect soups and sauces. This one has a 1950s look that conjures up images of cocktails and milkshakes as well. If you enjoy drinking fresh orange juice, invest in a stylish citrus press (below).

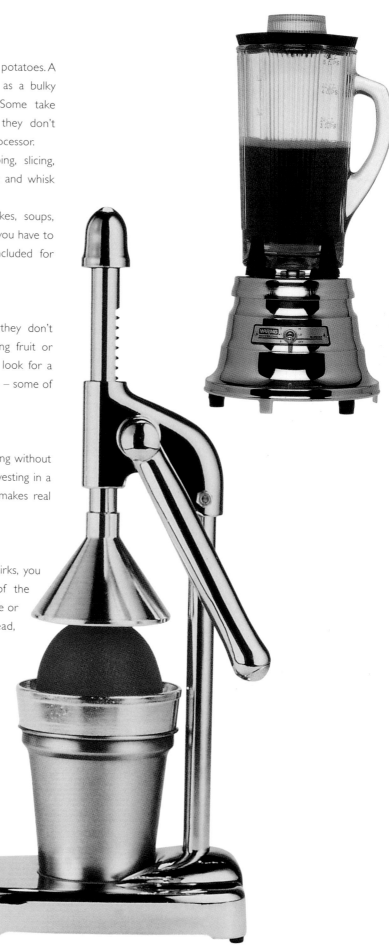

EQUIPMENT & ACCESSORIES

When you've never had to consider such things as kitchen accessories and cleaning equipment, it can come as a surprise that there are so many types available; from a comfortable distance, you may have assumed that one saucepan or vacuum cleaner was much the same as another. In some cases, the differences between one choice and another are large and fundamental; sometimes they are much more to do with personal preference. Across the board, though, the relevant information is perfectly straightforward and easy to understand.

saucepans

This is one area where your choice will be strongly influenced by how serious you are about cooking. Whichever type you choose, buy your pans individually rather than in a graduated set, even one that comes in a smart display rack. As Delia Smith points out in *How to Cook: Book One*, comparatively small pans are used most frequently and this is even more true when you're starting out. So invest in, say, two small pans and one medium one. Then, on the odd occasion you need something larger, you can always borrow it.

The fundamental difference between one saucepan and another is the material it's been manufactured from:

- **Enamelled steel** pans are cheap and light, and they come in bright colours. They are poor conductors of heat, though, and they stain and chip easily.
- **Non-stick** saucepans in their familiar form are a sensible choice for beginners. Convenient to use, they conduct heat well, they are excellent for people on low-fat diets and they are reasonably priced. For those with culinary aspirations, though, they have several drawbacks: they can be damaged by extremes of temperature and they should never be heated when empty. Metal implements scratch the surface, so use only wooden or plastic ones, and never attack the lining with an abrasive pad or powder. Recent technology has produced superior aluminium and stainless steel saucepans with a more resilient non-stick lining fired onto the base, but these cost much more than conventional non-stick ranges.
- **Stainless steel** pans offer fabulous and fashionable good looks. On its own, though, stainless steel is a poor conductor of heat and very hard to clean. Top-of-the-range brands have a sandwich of heavy aluminium, copper or silver alloy in the base, which improves conductivity.
- **Copper** pans have a burnished, almost painterly allure and they conduct heat briliantly, which is why you often see them in professional kitchens. Again, though, they have the double

downside that they are extremely expensive and very high maintenance. Modern copper saucepans are lined with stainless steel.

- **Heavy-gauge aluminium** is the best and most even conductor of heat and has a slight, natural non-stick quality. Its only disadvantage is that the surface can be attacked and discoloured by very acidic foods such as tomatoes and rhubarb.
- **Cast iron** is heavy and dense, and slow to take on or lose heat. This makes it perfect for long, slow cooking, or for searing food at high temperatures. A frying pan and a medium saucepan would be very useful, but don't try to cook with this material exclusively. Using a cast iron saucepan to heat a carton of soup, for example, wastes time and energy.

knives

Even cooks who have no time for high-tech machines and gadgets acknowledge the importance of good knives. You don't need many: a serrated bread knife, a carving knife (and fork), a couple of medium general-purpose knives and a small paring knife will do. You'll also need a steel to sharpen them. As you develop your culinary skills and interests, you can extend your collection further.

- **Carbon-steel** knives hold the sharpest edge but they need constant care since they have a tendency to rust easily.
- **Stainless steel** knives are much less demanding, and good-quality ones take an edge that is more than sharp enough for domestic purposes.
- **Ceramic** knives are actually made from a zirconium ceramic alloy developed for the aerospace industry. These blades are second only to diamonds in hardness and they stay sharp much longer than any metal. They are inexpensive, though, they have to be washed by hand, and they will chip or break if dropped.

BASIC KITCHEN EQUIPMENT

The following list includes most of the everyday utensils, gadgets, accessories and equipment you're likely to need. This is a very general, starter guide. If you're particularly interested in one aspect of cooking, such as baking cakes or making pastry, you'll need a special range of tools and accessories. Use these suggestions as a checklist, mentally discounting the things you know you won't use and adding anything you particularly depend on:

- wooden spoons of different sizes
- mixing bowls (two or three of different sizes)
- rubber spatula
- stainless steel tongs
- large serving and draining spoon
- fan (or petal) steamer, which adjusts to fit pans of different sizes
- flat turning slice
- pepper grinder
- lemon squeezer
- box grater
- mandolin slicer
- colander and sieve
- tin/bottle opener
- corkscrew
- vegetable peeler
- kitchen scissors (for bacon and fresh herbs as well as packets)
- balloon whisk
- bulb baster
- measuring spoons, jugs, cups and scales
- heavy-gauge stainless steel or aluminium baking tray and roasting pan
- baking dishes and casseroles
- glass storage jars for things like flour, sugar and tea that should be kept airtight
- oven mitts or gloves
- tea towels (about six including one linen cloth for glasses), preferably simple and similar in design rather than a collection of novelty souvenirs
- hand towels (two or three)

BASIC CLEANING EQUIPMENT

When it comes to housekeeping, the only major appliance you need is a vacuum cleaner. In terms of shape, there have always been two basic types: uprights and cylinders. At one time, they operated in slightly different ways. Although both use suction, all uprights had a beater bar (a rotating brush) as well to loosen the dirt. Beater bars are very effective on cut pile carpets, but they can damage loop piles and natural flooring such as coir and sisal, as well as polished floors.

Modern vacuum cleaners offer a wider choice since the beater bars on many uprights can be switched off, while some cylinders, although they don't have a beater bar, take a turbo brush attachment that does exactly the same job. As long as the model you choose is suitable for the surfaces you want to clean, you can base your selection on convenience (uprights are much easier to manoeuvre around large rooms, while cylinders with attachments are particularly good for awkward corners and stairs), ease of storage or just personal preference. A long extension lead will make life easier, whichever type you choose.

The other significant development in vacuum-cleaner technology is the emergence of the bagless model, which collects the dust in a removable canister instead of a disposable bag. Like traditional cleaners, however, these still have replaceable filters.

If, instead of large areas of carpet, you have mainly hard floors with rugs on top, consider one of the new stick cleaners, which are designed to cope with both surfaces. Light and easy to use, these look rather like a broom with a motor. Use one head for vacuuming rugs, then replace it with a felt pad to polish the hard flooring underneath. Finally, if you suffer from allergies or have pets, you may like to consider one of the specialist cleaners designed to deal with the most common triggers, like pet hair, dust mites and pollen.

This page: Hard-working equipment doesn't have to be dull. Choose a broom with yellow bristles and a grassy green handle and a vacuum with purple-and-silver livery.

Opposite: These delightful scales are perfect for modest kitchens, where they won't take up too much valuable work space and for cooks who don't take their food too seriously.

tools & supplies

Again, use this list as a basis for creating your own.

- sponge mop for washable floors
- plastic or metal bucket
- dustpan and brush (if your kitchen is big, a broom would be useful as well)
- dusters (soft purpose-made ones are much more efficient than old rags)
- general cleaning cloths and sponges (these should be washed and replaced regularly)
- dishwashing brush
- disposable dishcloths and scouring pads
- toothbrush (an old one is very useful for getting into nooks and crannies)

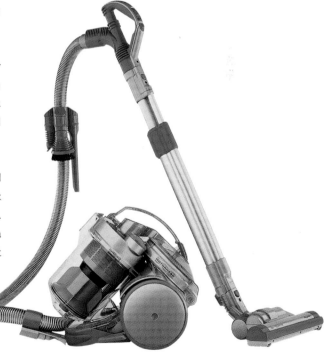

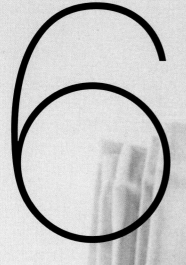

6

Sharing food with family and friends is one of the most companionable and rewarding of all social rituals. Whether you intend to eat in a separate dining room or a corner of your living room or kitchen, planning the area sensibly, and choosing suitable and well-designed furnishings

dining

areas

will encourage people to linger and chat long after all the plates have been cleared away. China, glass, cutlery and linen are equally important elements of a stylish and comfortable dining environment; finding out which items you are most likely to need, and what your options are in terms of sizes, shapes and materials, will help you to choose wisely.

PLANNING

If you have no interest in preparing food or entertaining on a formal basis, you may consider a dining area completely unnecessary, believing firmly that you'll be perfectly happy with a tray on your lap in front of the television. Even when you're sharing a takeaway with one or two friends, though, sitting around a table, no matter how simple, creates a unique spirit of conviviality – and it's also much more convenient and comfortable. What's more, a sturdy surface of standard working/dining height is extremely useful for activities such as paperwork, games and hobbies as well as for serving meals.

making space

Few first homes are likely to have a dedicated dining room; in most cases, meals are served either in a corner of the living room or in the kitchen, on a table that does double duty as a worktop. The only other option might be to take an otherwise wasted space, such as a large entrance hall or wide corridor, and try to squeeze in a small or narrow table. As a general rule, you should leave a space of at least 900 mm (36 in) between your dining table and the nearest wall for ease of use, and more between the table and a piece of furniture such as a sideboard or a dresser with drawers or doors that open out. One way of providing an occasional dining surface without encroaching too much on the surrounding space might be to arrange your room so the table, by itself, sits right against a wall, where it can act as a desk, or a home for your drinks tray. Then store your dining chairs elsewhere. Those with a suitable look can be assigned to alternative roles: if there are four, for example, two might act as occasional seating near the sofa, one could be a repository for discarded clothes in the bedroom and the other might provide a useful surface for post and packages in the hall. Folding or stacking chairs, on the other hand, could disappear altogether into a cupboard. When you want to serve a formal meal, clear the table, pull it out into the room and assemble all the chairs around it.

Whichever room you eat in, try to provide flooring that will not be ruined if a glass or a plate is accidentally knocked over; when you say to a mortified guest, 'Please don't worry

– no harm done,' it's always nice if you mean it. In the kitchen, of course, the floor will be washable anyway, but if your dining table sits on a pale carpet or an easily stained natural floor covering, consider defining the area with a large rug – perhaps an inexpensive cotton one that blends in unobtrusively. That way, if disaster does strike or you want a change, then you can always replace it without serious inconvenience or expense.

lighting

One of the main elements of a warm and intimate atmosphere is soft lighting, which is why – long after the invention of electricity – candles remain so strongly associated with a stylish table. There's no need to create an elaborate centrepiece with them, though, or to acquire formal holders: plain candles that are chunky enough to sit firmly on a plate or saucer will bathe everything in a flattering radiance and glimmer irresistibly on polished glass and china. (Those who are particularly given to visual drama might even consider a candle wall sconce or a simple candle chandelier made from brass or cast iron.)

One very practical option is a low pendant fitting, perhaps with a rise-and-fall mechanism and/or a dimmer switch so it can provide bright, general illumination for setting the table, and a more gentle, focussed pool of light during the meal as well. If that's not possible, a nearby wall or table lamp would achieve a similar effect. This type of flexibility is particularly invaluable when your dining table is in the kitchen; once the food is served, you can then cast the appliances, equipment and work surfaces into shadow and highlight only the dining area and the company.

Opposite: In this cool, open-plan loft, a simple rectangular table seats six for intimate gatherings. When numbers swell, its capacity can be increased by means of a central aluminium leaf. The supporting struts and the detailing on the legs are also aluminium, and the central supports of the spherical rise-and-fall pendants reinforce the metallic theme. Note the slim tile border that expands the room visually by extending the floor surface up to skirting-board height.

FURNITURE

When fast food restaurants depend on a high turnover of customers, they install tables and chairs specially designed to be comfortable for only a very limited time. After that, the occupants invariably begin to shift and squirm, and before long, they get up and leave. Unless you want the appeal of your dining area to have the same limited duration, consider the ergonomics just as carefully as the appearance of its most important furnishings.

tables

The key elements here are size, shape, support and height. As a general guide, each person needs about 700 mm (28 in) to wield cutlery without banging the elbows of the next diner. A small round or square table will seat a maximum of four people; if floor space is restricted, look for one that folds up flat. To feed six, you'll need a bigger round surface or a rectangular design. Once you get into larger numbers, a rectangle – with or without removable leaves – is the most practical choice. This is largely because the elegant democracy of a round surface (everyone can talk to everyone else and no-one is seated at the 'head') becomes impractical when, in order to provide enough space around the outside, the diameter is so vast that not only are you unable to converse across it comfortably, but it also takes up a huge amount of room.

Another feature to look for is the way in which your table is supported: square and rectangular designs that have legs at each corner present no problem, and round tables on a pedestal base are ideal (although the pressure exerted on the rim of a large, round top when several people lean on it continually tends to produce an unsettling degree of wobble). Some types of surface though – those that extend by means of a flap, a gate-leg structure or a series of leaves, or large, round tables with legs instead of a central pedestal – impose their own limitations on the number of places you can set without requiring some of your guests to straddle a support awkwardly.

Most dining tables are about 760 mm (30 in) high, but they all differ widely when it comes to the thickness of the

Above: Strong Japanese influences have produced this dramatic dining area dominated by a huge lacquer-black table, paper-shaded lamp and woven stools, which replace conventional chairs.

Above left: Find a dining chair you like, and take home one in every colour instead of a matching set.

Left: When your dinner parties are very occasional, invest in an adjustable table that you can raise from coffee to dining height. Make sure the one you choose operates quickly and easily, though.

top or the depth of the border or edging strip, so make sure you test any prospective purchase first to see whether your thighs tuck comfortably underneath; if you like to sit with your legs crossed, make sure that position is possible too. When you're shopping for a table to go with chairs you already own, take the trouble to measure one of them to determine the distance from the floor to the seat and keep a note of it; you can then road-test the tables you like best using a chair of a similar height.

The most popular material for dining surfaces is wood, sometimes with a laminate or sheet metal veneer. The other option that might tempt you is a glass top, but many people find this an impractical choice since glass not only shows every smear and scratch, it also contributes to disconcertingly noisy mealtimes when plates, cutlery and glasses clatter on its hard finish. Ceramic tile surfaces have similar drawbacks, and they tend to collect dirt and stains in their grouting.

individual, but closely related ones, so apply this principle to a junk-shop search for more contemporary designs. Choose a selection of visually compatible bentwood chairs, for example, or those styled in wicker, tubular steel (combined with leather, canvas or cane), or moulded plastic or ply.

If your chairs have an upholstered seat and/or back, minimize work and worry by avoiding very expensive covering fabrics or those that can't be sponged with water, and as soon as possible, treat them with a proprietary stain repellent.

Finally, no matter how pressed you are for space, try not to solve the problem with bench seating. Perching on a hard, narrow surface without any back support will leave your guests longing to leave the table well before they've even finished the main course.

storage

Unless you are starting out with two complete sets of tableware, one for everyday and the other for special occasions, you are unlikely to need extensive storage facilities near the dining table (unless, of course, your kitchen is so tiny that keeping most of your glass and china elsewhere would be a wise plan). What would be very useful, though, especially when you entertain at a fairly small table, is an adjacent surface for wine and water bottles, serving dishes and plates, and condiments. The standard furnishing items designed to fulfil this function are the sideboard and the dresser, and neither should be dismissed purely on the grounds of its traditional nature. A deep, solid shelf would do the job just as well, though – or use a shallow console table or even a wide, medium-height chest of drawers, which would also provide a home for tablecloths and napkins, heatproof mats, cutlery and candles.

If no amount of skilful planning will free enough space for a permanent serving surface, consider using a wheeled trolley – perhaps one you can borrow from the kitchen or home office. Light years removed in aesthetic terms from the heated hostess trolleys of the 1960s, this functional, multi-purpose item allows you to serve second helpings and fill empty glasses conveniently, without either overloading the dining table or being forced to dash constantly back and forth to the kitchen throughout the meal.

chairs

As well as providing a padded surface to sit on, a dining chair should support your thighs and your back without digging into either of them. Most have seats about 400 mm (16 in) from the floor, but it's probably more useful to aim for a gap of about 300 mm (12 in) between the surface of the seat and the underside of the table top (or the bottom of any edging strip). Again, try to test all your potential purchases with a table the same height as your own. If you plan to invest in chairs with arms, make sure they will tuck neatly under the table surface between meals.

There's no need for your dining chairs to match, but they should have a basic sympathy in style, shape and proportion. As any antique enthusiast is aware, an identical set of period chairs costs considerably more than the same number of

This page: For those who wouldn't give house room to anything as trad as a sideboard, this anodized aluminium cupboard is the perfect techno-chic storage solution.

Opposite: Up to six of these lightweight chairs in fruit-jelly colours can be stacked in a single pile.

TABLEWARE

The days are long past when one of the seminal images connected with setting up home was a bride choosing her 'best' china, glass, cutlery and table linen. In the modern world, few people have either the money or the space for two sets of tableware and in any case, the life we lead is much less compartmentalized than it was even a generation ago. We now entertain more often, but less formally, with intimate, relaxed suppers taking the place of hidebound dinner parties.

Most people (certainly most young people) use the same plates, glasses and forks for everything from quick snacks to Christmas dinner, so the designs you choose have to be supremely adaptable as well as pleasing to your eye. The overall look you choose for your table is likely to have a strong affinity with the one you create in your rooms: sleek designer modern, catering/no-frills, natural/handmade, stylized Art Deco, elaborate Victorian, etc.

There's no need for all the elements to come in complete sets; if you're drawn to a retro look, it's often more interesting and personal to collect single, sympathetic pieces from junk shops and markets, but if you do this with one or two elements, keep the others plain and matching. Team odd glasses (engraved tumblers, maybe, or chunky wine glasses) and cutlery (with curvy, period handles, say, or ivory-hued bone ones) with china that is all one pattern, and a simple, coordinated cloth and napkins. Or collect flowery, blue-and-white or spotted china and embroidered or checked table linen, and team them with low-key, matching glass and cutlery.

If your finances are restricted, start with only those items you'll use on a regular basis. Once in a while, if you decide to throw a drinks party or invite a huge crowd of friends round for supper, you can always hire or borrow anything else.

china

To cope with everyday meals and informal entertaining, a practical collection of china to begin with might include:

- dinner plates
- side/dessert plates
- bowls (choose a size that you can use for cereal, soup and fruit or dessert)
- cups and saucers (if you use them), or mugs
- a teapot is essential to the functioning of many households: choose one that matches your china or a plain one, which is likely to be much less expensive

Later on, you can add smaller (or larger) bowls, coffee cups and saucers, open or covered serving dishes, oval platters, two or three jugs (for cream, milk, sauces and gravy) and any other specialist items that appeal.

CARING FOR CHINA
- Never store plates or bowls in towering stacks; pulling items out from the middle or bottom of a pile increases the risk of chips and cracks.
- Don't hang fragile old cups by the handle.
- As long as there is no delicate or handpainted decoration involved, you can often remove stains by soaking in proprietary stain remover, biological washing powder or denture cleaner. Everyday white earthenware will come clean in a weak solution of household bleach.
- If you intend putting your china in a dishwasher, then always make sure the range you choose is 'dishwasher proof' as opposed to 'dishwasher resistant', which suggests the pattern is likely to fade gradually over the years.

Opposite: Plain, elegant tableware will add a strong sense of style to the simplest meal, and boost your confidence significantly if you haven't had much experience of entertaining.

Plain, and especially white, off-white or cream, earthenware is less expensive than heavily decorated ranges. With a timelessly stylish appeal, it adapts readily to any degree of formality, and – perhaps most significantly – it never competes for attention with the food.

There are several ways to buy new china: as single pieces, in individual place settings, or in starter sets that contain four or six place settings, and sometimes include a few serving items. These starter sets usually sell for considerably less than the combined price of the individual items, and can offer excellent value. If you can't afford to buy everything at once, it's probably more useful to collect what you need item by item, rather than in place settings. So, instead of starting off with two place settings, go for perhaps four dinner plates and four bowls, then add side plates, cups and saucers, separate soup plates, etc. as you can afford them. Unless the pattern you've chosen is a classic that's been on the market for decades, it might be worth asking how long the manufacturer plans to keep it in production (some guarantee a minimum period); bear in mind that very trendy colours and designs may be discontinued within a year or two, which means that even if you've acquired all the items you want, you won't be able to replace any breakages.

As well as traditional outlets, explore catering supply companies; their crockery may not be cheaper (and it's unlikely to be available in starter sets), but it will withstand a great deal of rough treatment and tends to come in classic shapes and include desirable items such as vast dinner plates and generous breakfast cups and saucers. Or explore your local outlet for second-quality china (known as 'seconds'). Supplies are, by definition, irregular, so when you see something you really like, snap it up immediately. The prices are often astoundingly low, though, and any imperfections virtually undetectable.

Some auction houses, too, regularly offer complete (or nearly complete) sets of china in excellent condition at a fraction of the price you'd pay for the same items new. This is a particularly attractive option if you want a traditional or period look for your table – although, surprisingly often, the 'period' of the patterns on offer is the 1970s or 1980s.

GLOSSARY

Although the general term 'china' tends to be used for all types of ceramic ware (the word 'ceramic' indicates clay-based material fired in a kiln), there are actually four different types in common use:

- **Earthenware**, the most widely used for inexpensive domestic tableware, is made from a mixture of clay and stone. It is opaque and whitish in colour and in its natural state, porous, which is why it is usually glazed. Because they are made for hotels and restaurants, some earthenware ranges are thicker than their domestic equivalents, with rolled edges that resist chipping. These ranges are known as 'vitreous hotelware' and 'vitrified' means fired at a high temperature to make the items non-porous.

- **Stoneware** has the same components as earthenware, but in slightly different proportions, which give it an opaque grey or brown colour. Fired at a higher temperature than earthenware, stoneware is non-porous, and is sometimes used for baking dishes as well as tableware.

- **Porcelain** is a general term for white, vitrified pottery that is translucent in appearance rather than opaque, yet exceptionally fine and strong.

- **Bone china** is similar to porcelain: white, fine, translucent, non-porous and strong at the same time. Its composition includes 50 per cent bone ash (primarily cattle bone, burnt and ground into powder).

This page and opposite: Invest in a collection of relatively cheap drinking glasses for everyday use and casual entertaining so you don't have to worry about accidental breakages. If you can afford (or if you're given) an expensive set, or you inherit the family crystal, save it for those extra-special occasions.

glass

A few basic shapes and sizes of drinking glass will cover almost every eventuality:

- hi-ball or water glasses
- tumblers
- stemmed wine glasses
- smaller stemmed glasses
- champagne flutes

Always choose clear drinking glasses, since coloured ones distort the appearance of the liquid, a disadvantage that is particularly relevant for wine drinkers. You can buy wine glasses in a variety of different sizes and shapes, but all you really need to start out with are medium-to-largish ones for white and good red wine (red table wine is equally at home in tumblers), smaller stemmed ones to hold sherry, port and liqueur, and champagne flutes, if possible. As well as adding a celebratory air to any kind of occasion, flutes enhance your enjoyment of sparkly wine by preserving its magical bubbles (unlike old-fashioned champagne coupes, whose shallow, flattish shape has the very opposite effect).

All wine glasses should curve in slightly at the top to prevent the contents from spilling as you swirl it expertly around the bowl to release its fragrant bouquet, and to contain as much of that intoxicating bouquet as possible. Also, to appreciate the colour and concentration of a good wine more fully, always serve it in unadorned, clear glasses rather than any elaborately cut, etched or heavily patterned ones.

Because glass is so much more fragile than earthenware or porcelain, you're less likely to find complete sets of antique tumblers, water or wine glasses at auction or on market stalls, but attractive, single examples are well worth seeking out.

CARING FOR GLASS

- When you wash up by hand, deal with the glasses first, while the water is clean and hot. If you don't have a draining rack, rest them on a soft cloth on the draining board, then polish them with a linen tea towel.
- Try soaking glass that has become stained in a solution of biological washing powder.
- The commonly held notion that glasses should be stored upside-down 'to keep out the dust' is, in fact, deeply misguided. Not only is this unnecessary (everyday glasses don't sit still long enough to become dusty, while those used infrequently should be rinsed before use anyway), but it seriously weakens the rims and makes them much more vulnerable to chipping.
- Handpainted or delicate glass, particularly if it's hand-blown, is unlikely to be suitable for machine washing. Most ordinary glasses can be treated in this way, however, but always follow the manufacturer's instructions when it comes to things like detergent, temperature and recommended additives such as salt and water softener.

GLOSSARY

Glassware is categorized by its manufacturing process, its composition, or both:

- **Pressed glass** is made by forming molten glass into the required shape in a two-part mould. This type of glass is generally the cheapest.

- **Mouth-blown glass** is formed by taking up a lump (called a 'gob') of molten glass on the end of a tube, then blowing it into a bubble and shaping it by hand using a number of specialist tools.

- **Machine-blown glass** involves the same process as mouth-blown glass, but in a fully automated form.

- **Cut glass** is decorated with a pattern of deep, straight grooves cut into the surface of the glass with a wheel after it has been formed.

- **Engraved glass** is marked in a similar way, but features thinner lines, some of which are curved. Fine engraving is sometimes carried out with a delicate pencil-like tool instead of a wheel.

- **Etched glass** is embellished by covering the surface with a protective layer of wax or rubber that leaves only the area to be decorated exposed. It is then immersed in etching acid, or sandblasted to give the same effect.

- **Soda-lime glass**, the type in general use, is suitable for all the manufacturing and decorating processes.

- **Lead crystal** and **full lead crystal** are both terms that indicate the presence of lead oxide, which makes glass less brittle and more light reflective, and therefore easier and more rewarding to cut. There is no universal standard to indicate what proportion of lead is suggested by each of these terms, but full lead crystal will contain more than lead crystal. Both types of crystal are much heavier and more expensive than ordinary glass.

cutlery

A basic set should include:

- table knives and forks
- dessert knives and forks (also used for starters)
- dessert spoons (which can double as soup spoons)
- tea spoons
- table or serving spoons

When you can afford more, you might add soup spoons, extra dessert knives and forks for when you need them at both ends of the meal, more serving spoons, salad servers (or use two tablespoons) and specialist implements such as a gravy ladle or cheese knife.

Finally, least expensive and most widely used of all is stainless-steel cutlery, while silver plate and solid silver are extremely expensive and they require a great deal of tender and time-consuming care. Stainless-steel ranges are created in almost every design imaginable, but it's a wise move to avoid florid period patterns that were quite clearly conceived with precious metals in mind; it's best to stick to more restrained, timeless shapes or simple, modern ones. Some designs are made up of stainless steel throughout, while others have plastic, ceramic or wooden handles: many of these are unsuitable for dishwashers, so always check before you buy. When you find a range you especially like, hold each piece in your hand to check that it feels comfortable and is not too heavy, or badly balanced.

Once again, catering suppliers are well worth investigating for ranges of stainless-steel cutlery. If you long for the elegance of silver, though, and your budget won't stretch to a new set, choose a classic design (like Kings or Rattail) and scour markets, antique shops and car boot sales for small bundles or even single examples.

Opposite: Look for odd glasses from your favourite period. Shown here, from the top, are an Art Deco cocktail glass, a 1960s hi-ball (with swizzle sticks) and a 1950s champagne coupe. According to legend, this shape was modelled on one of Marie Antoinette's breasts.

This page: Simple, elegant cutlery in top-quality stainless steel suits any style or occasion and lasts for decades.

CARING FOR CUTLERY

- Rinse your cutlery immediately, and wash it as soon as possible after use since some foods (those containing vinegar, lemon juice or egg, for example) can cause staining and pitting, even on stainless steel.
- Even if you don't own a dishwasher, never leave cutlery with wooden, bone, plastic, resin or ceramic handles to soak in water.
- If you have any silver or silver-plated items, store them separately since they will easily scratch in the rough-and-tumble of a general cutlery drawer.
- Stainless-steel spoons stained with tea will come clean if you soak them in a mild solution of household bleach.

CARING FOR TABLE LINEN

- The key to all effective stain removal is prompt action, so avoid the temptation to put off dealing with spills until the following day.
- Small splashes of red wine are easier to remove when you sprinkle them immediately with enough table salt to absorb the excess.
- White cotton and linen respond well to a mild bleach solution, but don't try this on coloured or printed fabrics.

table linen

To protect your table, help deaden the clatter of plates and glasses, and give an individual touch to your setting, cover the surface with a cloth or placemats of some kind. The selection available is enormous.

For everyday meals, especially if the room you eat in has a generally informal look, consider a cloth of wipeable PVC-covered cotton, which is made in a huge range of plain colours and gorgeous patterns – flowery, graphic, retro or funky. Or keep one or two coloured or printed cloths for all your casual meals, and perhaps just one formal cloth (plain and pale; damask if you prefer a traditional look) for any special-occasion entertaining.

Make an effort to provide generously sized fabric napkins for shared evening meals, even your more relaxed suppers with friends. At lunch time, paper napkins – as long as they're strong and thick – are fine. If you don't like any of the conventional napkins available, improvise by buying large, old-fashioned men's handkerchiefs to use instead – or small headscarves, perhaps in a cheerful border print or lively pattern of spots.

Tablecloths, napkins and placemats, whatever their style, should be made from a natural fibre such as cotton or linen. Synthetics, even when blended with cotton, hold onto stains – especially grease stains – tenaciously, and can also have an unfortunate clammy feel.

setting the table

The conventional placement of china, glass and cutlery on a dining table is not a complex and meaningless exercise in social ritual; it's a logical way of organizing these items so they're convenient and comfortable to use.

Forks always go on the left, spoons and knives (with their blades facing inward) on the right. Place cutlery in the order in which it will be used throughout the meal, working from the outside in. So, if your first course is soup, the soup spoon should be on the outside; if your starter requires a small knife and fork, they will go there instead. Next come the dinner knife and fork, and then, closest to the plate, whatever implements are needed for dessert.

Glasses go on the right of the place setting, just above the knife or knives, water glass to the right of the wine glass. Side plates go on the left, beside the forks. If you're serving salad with a cold meal, it can be placed directly on the dinner plate. When the meal is hot, provide a separate bowl or plate for salad, and put it above the side plate on the left. Napkins can either be folded on the side plates or the dinner plates (if you're placing these on the table as opposed to dishing up the food elsewhere).

Right: Set the mood of your meals with your table linen. Here, the bright blue cloth and napkins with their subtle woven check establish a fresh, casual feeling. Set out on pale damask, however, the same china and cutlery would look more formal.

Opposite: Some kitchen and dining tables have a drawer at one end to store cutlery neatly and safely away. Note the stripy cotton runner, which protects the surface of the table without covering it completely.

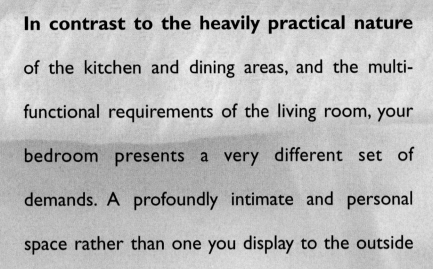

7

In contrast to the heavily practical nature of the kitchen and dining areas, and the multi-functional requirements of the living room, your bedroom presents a very different set of demands. A profoundly intimate and personal space rather than one you display to the outside

bedrooms

world, it should not only represent the embodiment of your own tastes and priorities, it should also offer you peace, privacy and restorative ease at the end of even the most stressful days. The most vital function of any bedroom is to provide a healthy and comfortable place to sleep; most also contain storage space for clothing and accessories, and some include a dedicated surface for grooming as well.

PLANNING

As with any other domestic area, planning a bedroom involves assessing your space, then thinking about the various functions and furnishings you will want to fit in it. For example, if you already own a bed, how big is it? If you're planning to buy one, what size would you like it to be? Look closely at your storage requirements: are we talking about a comprehensive collection of garments or a capsule wardrobe? Are any of your possessions particularly space-consuming — bulky hat boxes, maybe, or a serious accumulation of shoes? Do you want a surface in your bedroom to use as a dressing table, a writing desk — or both? What about chairs: a small one to drape clothing over and/or an easy chair you can curl up in? This kind of decision often revolves around the make-up of the household. If there are two people who relax in different ways, a quiet corner away from the television may alleviate a certain amount of friction.

When you have a rough idea of all the items you will need, start thinking about where they might go, bearing in mind the surrounding space which each one requires for safe and comfortable use. If you want your bed to project into the room, for instance, allow a corridor around it of about 750 mm (30 in). Allow 950 mm (37 in) if any doors open

An adaptable Venetian blind, recessed wall spots and a pair of graphic vertical radiators ensure a comfortable level of light and heat in this Art Deco-inspired bedroom

into the same space. A chest of drawers requires exactly the same amount of clearance – 950 mm (37 in) – in front, while a dressing table requires 600 mm (24 in) for a chair to be pulled in and out comfortably.

One way of maximizing space is by tucking the bed in a corner so one side is against a wall; if you do this, make sure your bed is on castors so you can pull it out easily to make it and to clean underneath. Don't choose a wall that's shared with noisy neighbours, and avoid any position near a draughty window.

The atmosphere you create in your bedroom should be harmonious; base your scheme around shades and textures that make you feel calm and secure. Because it looks and feels cosy underfoot, carpet is the most popular flooring in bedrooms. In most cases, too, it's more affordable here than in a living room of a similar size since, unless you have plans to create a busy, multi-purpose space, you can make do with a less durable grade. If your heart is set on a hardwood floor, adding a rug beside the bed would at least provide a soft surface to step onto first thing in the morning. Be careful, though, of softwood floorboards, which splinter easily and can inflict nasty wounds on unprotected flesh.

At the window (or windows), the most important practical consideration here is whether your curtains or blinds will dim the light sufficiently for you to sleep past dawn, and snooze in the afternoon whenever you feel the need. At the same time, they should admit enough daylight so you can identify the contents of your wardrobe and drawers, check your image in a full-length mirror, and see clearly enough to shave or apply your make-up.

After dark, you'll need artificial illumination that will fulfil the same functions, plus task lighting beside the bed. If there are two of you, choose fittings that direct their light so one person can read without disturbing the other. For a calming touch, put a drop of lavender oil on the bulb.

Above right: In your private sanctuary, surround yourself with colours that make you feel relaxed. Blue is one of the most popular choices for this room

Right: Provide a bedside unit to keep necessities close by. Here, the top holds a lamp, clock and reading matter while drawers store bits and pieces.

CHOOSING YOUR BED

Buying a bed may not be as inspiring as shopping for more glamorous items, but it's worth taking time over since you spend a third of your life there. The quality of your bed has a profound effect on the quality of your sleep, and this directly affects both your physical and mental well-being.

First, dismiss all thoughts of acquiring a second-hand bed. Most beds have a lifespan of about ten years only, but even if a bed is not completely worn out, it will fail to support your body properly since it will have moulded itself to the shape of its previous occupant. An even more alarming factor is hygiene; every year, about 50 litres (87.5 pints) of perspiration and 500 grammes (1 pound) of skin cells disappear into your mattress. Are you really prepared to sleep on one that belonged to someone else?

bed basics

Most people sleep on a sprung mattress, which rests either on a sprung base, or a more solid base of wooden slats or sometimes wire mesh. A sprung base costs more but it will also provide the best support; a slatted or mesh base (which usually comes as part of a bedstead with side rails and head and foot boards) may give less substantial support, but it will allow more ventilation, which may well be a worthwhile trade-off for allergy or asthma sufferers. A warning note: never put a new mattress on an old base: they are made to function together, so if the base is saggy and lumpy, an expensive new mattress will quickly begin to feel the same.

Sprung bases are available in two main types: sprung-edge and firm-edge. Sprung-edge bases, the most luxurious, have a layer of springs mounted on top of their wooden frame, which give the bed a similar degree of 'give' all over its surface. The advantage of these extra springs is that they make the bed more durable and improve its ventilation. In a firm-edge base, the wooden frame has no springs on top, and is therefore hard and unyielding around the perimeter. This can be a plus point for those who, perhaps because of disability or injury, find it awkward to get in and out of bed, and appreciate this extra stability. Because there are fewer springs, this type of base often costs less than the sprung-edge version. Another feature to look out for in a bed base is storage capacity, in the form of either drawers or a roomy compartment that you reach by lifting up a hinged mattress. This extra facility adds to the cost of the bed and tends to increase its height, but when space is scarce, it can be invaluable.

When it comes to the mattress itself, there are three main types of springing: 'open' springing, 'linked' springing and 'pocketed' springing. The disadvantage of the first two systems is that the springs are joined, so that when pressure is placed on one, its neighbours are pulled down as well to form a depression under the

Above: Expand your storage capacity by choosing a divan bed with drawers in its base. Drawer divans tend to be about 60 mm (2½ in) higher than standard models.

Opposite: Contemporary bedrooms offer clean lines as well as comfort. Here, a tailored headboard and flat valance replace the more traditional excesses of quilted satin and enveloping frills.

sleeper; if the bed has two occupants, the lighter one tends to roll toward the heavier. 'Individual' or 'pocketed' springs cost more than more rudimentary versions, but their superior construction (opposite page) reduces this problem. Some pocketed springs are joined only at the waist, and these have the greatest degree of independent movement.

Sprung mattresses have several layers of padding on top. These consist of coarse materials such as horsehair, sisal or coir, and soft ones like wool, felt, foam and polyester, which lie directly under the cover.

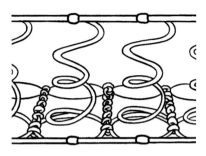

Open springing is made up of rows of separate, hourglass-shaped springs joined with wire at both top and bottom. This type is usually the least expensive option.

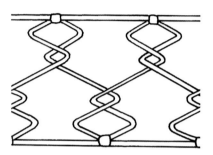

Linked springing is slightly more costly than open springing and involves a continuous run of springs made from a single, long piece of wire, rather like knitting.

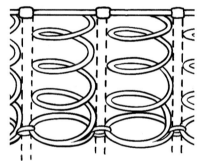

Pocketed springing offers greater support than either of the above because each spring is enclosed in a separate fabric pocket, which increases its capacity for independent movement.

Above: The degree of firmness you require in your bed is largely a matter of personal preference. On the whole, though, the less you weigh, the more rigid any mattress will feel. Unfortunately, apparently technical terms such as 'orthopaedic', while usually denoting a hardish mattress or base, are largely meaningless, since different manufacturers use them to indicate various levels of firmness.

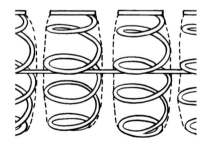

Barrel-shaped pocketed springing has rings that telescope inside one another to reduce noise and wear. The best pocketed springs (of either shape) are joined only at the waist.

SHOPPING TIPS

Before you can come to a valid judgement, you will need to test any prospective purchase by lying full out on it for several minutes. Perching on the edge or prodding it with your finger will not tell you anything. One useful exercise is to lie face-up on the bed and slip your hand underneath the small of your back. If you can get it in easily, the bed is too hard; if you can't get it in at all, the bed is too soft. The right mattress will support you firmly so that you can turn easily, with your hips and shoulders gently cradled.

If there are two of you, and you are vastly different in weight (or have opposing preferences in terms of firmness), consider buying two single beds that zip together. If you decide on a double, buy the biggest (and if necessary, the longest) one you can afford. At the very least, your bed should be wide enough to allow the two of you to lie side by side with your hands behind your heads and without your elbows touching. Remember that even if you normally sleep wrapped round each other, there will be times when one person is restless, ill or needing space. And if you're on your own, a small double bed offers more room to manoeuvre than a single one.

variations on a theme

After sprung beds, one of the most popular choices is foam beds, usually made from high-quality latex, which also provides excellent support and durability. Foam beds are particularly suitable for allergy sufferers; they don't contain natural fillings such as wool that may trigger an attack, and are less likely to harbour dust mites.

Another widely available option is a futon, a non-sprung pad filled with layers of cotton, wool, or man-made fibres. The advantage of a futon is that it can be rolled up and put away when it's not in use. On the down side, futons are very hard, since they are designed for use on either the floor or a specially constructed timber base. In addition, they need to be shaken and ventilated regularly.

Less common and generally more expensive than any of the above are water beds; these distribute your body weight evenly, with no pressure points, and they are also good for allergy sufferers. Most have an integral heating system so the water is maintained at a comfortable temperature. Apart from the initial cost, and the fact that some people have difficulty in adjusting to the rather strange sensation of sleeping on water, the main drawback with these beds is the actual weight of them. If you have one in mind for an upstairs bedroom, make certain your floor can support it first.

Left: For a cool, spare look, install a bed with a simple, low platform to support the mattress. This is much more sophisticated and considerably more comfortable than sleeping on the floor. In this otherwise austere chamber, note the control switch that suggests the presence of a cosy electric blanket.

Below: When you've finished your morning tea in bed, turn the covers back completely to air the sheets and the mattress. If you don't do this, the damp that has accumulated during the night has no chance to evaporate. Here, perfumed breezes enter the room through a large window overlooking the garden.

CARING FOR YOUR BED

- Never put a mattress directly on the floor. Without proper ventilation, it will soon develop mildew and start to smell musty. If you want the exotic effect of a low bed, place it on a raised platform drilled with large holes.

- Don't leave the protective wrapping on a new mattress or base. Again, moisture will be trapped inside and this will encourage damp.

- First thing in the morning, throw back the bedclothes and air the bed for at least 20 minutes before you make it.

- Every week for the first month, and then every three months after that, turn a sprung mattress over and reverse head and foot ends to help the filling settle evenly. (Foam beds don't require turning.) Try not to bend your mattress and remember that when you move house, it should never be rolled up and crammed into a van.

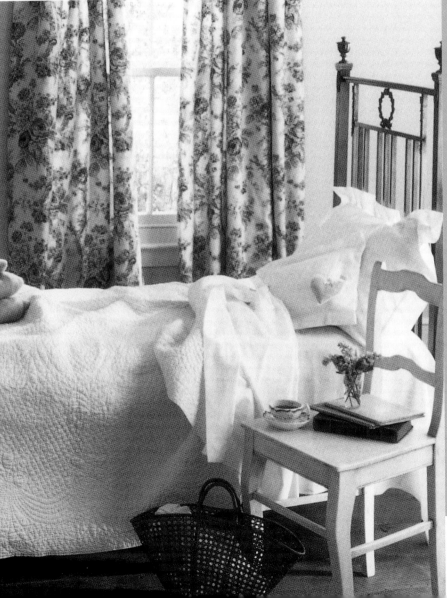

BEDLINEN

The items you'll need to stock your linen cupboard will depend on whether you prefer to sleep with a duvet or blanket and top sheet. Duvets have come to dominate the market over the last few decades because they're deliciously soft, light and warm to snuggle under. They also remove much of the drudgery from bedmaking and, although they have a higher unit price than blankets, duvets cost less to provide the same amount of warmth. Blankets score points with some traditionalists, however, who appreciate their simple lines and the visual appeal of a crisp sheet folded back over the edge. They are slightly more flexible in that you can pile them up when it's cold, and peel them off again when spring arrives, and those made of fine, downy wool provide the necessary tactile gratification for people who find the cosy plumpness of a duvet slightly suffocating.

choosing a duvet

The main difference between one duvet and another is what's inside: some have natural fillings while others are filled with a synthetic material such as polyester. Natural fillings are usually feather or down (duck or goose), or a combination of both. 'Feather and down' is the least expensive type and contains more of the former than the latter; 'down and feather' duvets cost more because they contain more down than feather. 'Pure goose down' is the highest-quality designation and therefore carries the highest price. Less common, and usually priced at the top end of the market, are duvets filled with cotton or wool. Some natural duvets can be washed in very large machines, while others must be dry cleaned using a specialist technique: check the care instructions to be certain.

Duvets filled with synthetic material (often polyester) are cheaper to buy, but they have a lower warmth-to-weight ratio. They are fully washable, though, and perfect for allergy sufferers.

Whichever filling you decide on, choose a duvet with a grid construction rather than a series of long channels that encourage the filling to gather at one end so you have to shake it down regularly. (The other advantage of this design is that if a small nick or tear is inflicted on the casing, the volume of feathers that can escape is limited.)

Duvets are graded according to insulation capacity, which effectively means warmth. Grading systems vary, but look for terms like 'tog' or 'fill-power'. If your requirements change dramatically from season to season, buy one with a high rating for winter, and replace it with a much lighter one (or a thin blanket) in the summer. Alternatively, choose an 'all seasons' set, which consists of a medium-weight and light-weight grade fastened together so you can use one or the other (or both) according to the weather.

An ivory jacquard weave links all the linen on this inviting bed: duvet cover, flat valance (just visible), and two styles of pillowcase. To complete the coordination, curtains and lampshade in the same fabric were purchased ready made.

For maximum comfort, invest in a larger duvet than is indicated for the size of your bed. If you sleep in a single bed, for example, go for a double duvet, and if two of you sleep together (especially if one or both are restless sleepers), consider having two separate duvets instead of one big one. Duvets vary hugely in terms of life expectancy: when yours becomes thinner and you feel less warm underneath, that's the time to replace it.

blankets

Here, natural fibres such as wool and cotton have a clear edge over synthetics in terms of both warmth and texture. Pure wool blankets are the lightest and warmest, while cellular blankets, which can either be made of wool or cotton, are useful as an extra warmth-trapping layer between an ordinary blanket and top sheet. To give a secure tuck-in all around, choose a blanket at least 750 mm (30 in) wider and 500 mm (20 in) longer than your mattress.

Those who are particularly sensitive to the cold often find an electric blanket extremely effective. There are two types: overblankets and underblankets. Overblankets go over a top sheet in the same way as ordinary blankets and they are usually left on all night. They shouldn't have any weight on top of them, though, even when they're turned off, so this limits your use of the bed during the day. Underblankets lie directly on top of the mattress and are intended to heat the bed before you get in. Although you can't lie on top of them when they're on high, most have one or two lower settings that can safely be left on all night. Avoid second-hand electric blankets and have yours serviced regularly.

pillows

Like duvets, pillows are filled with feathers and/or down or a man-made fibre such as polyester. Unless you are allergy prone, choosing between them is a matter of preference. It's worth noting, though, that top-quality synthetic fillings keep their shape best. Conventional pillows are rectangular; big, square ones are known as continental or European.

All pillows eventually lose their original shape and resilience, and using a thin, lumpy one can affect your sleep patterns significantly. If yours has been around for a while,

test it by holding your arm straight out in front of you and laying the pillow across it widthways. The pillow should maintain its basic shape, forming a gently obtuse angle over your arm. If it flops almost straight down at each side, though, it's in urgent need of replacement.

People who sleep on their back need to have only one pillow, while those who sleep on their side should have at least two so their head and neck are supported in alignment. If you suffer from any kind of neck or shoulder pain, investigate the benefits of a special support pillow designed to maintain a healthy posture.

Below: Learn to balance your chosen colours with neutral hues. Here, soft French blue is set off with white lace and a tumblerful of pale blooms.

linen
shopping list

Duvet devotees will need pillowcases, a bottom sheet and a duvet cover, while the blanket brigade should have pillowcases, a bottom sheet and a top sheet. As an optional extra in both camps, consider some kind of valance or skirt to hide the base of your bed when the covers are pulled back. For each bed that is slept in on a regular basis, you should have at least two full sets of linen: one in use and one in the wash.

- **Pillowcases** come without a border (called 'housewife' style) or with a plain, flat border ('Oxford' style).
- **Bottom sheets** are either standard flat sheets tucked in underneath the mattress, or special fitted sheets with elasticated corners. Fitted sheets are preferable to flat ones in that, instead of wrinkling up beneath you, they provide a taut, smooth surface, which is much nicer to sleep on and looks neater as well. Also, fitted sheets simplify bedmaking considerably, since they don't have to be straightened and tucked in again every day.
- **Top sheets** should be at least 610 mm (24 in) longer and wider than your bed to give a generous tuck-in.
- **Duvet covers** are like enormous bags with a long opening in one side. They differ from one another largely

in the way this opening is fastened: if possible, choose a simple device such as buttons or ties, which can be repaired easily. More sophisticated fastenings like zips or press studs are tedious to deal with if they break. (Useful tip: stitch a 20 cm [8 in] length of bias tape to the two inside corners of your cover opposite the opening, and on the two corresponding corners of your duvet. When you put a new cover on a duvet, begin by anchoring these two corners first to make the job more manageable.)

- **Valances** come slightly gathered or plain and flat with box pleats at each corner and sometimes one in the middle of each long side as well. Both these styles are attached to a fabric panel sandwiched between mattress and base.

Always buy bedlinen according to the actual measurements of your mattress since different manufacturers may use terms such as 'double' or 'king' to indicate different sizes.

fabrics
& fashions

No man-made fibre can duplicate the unmistakable smell and luxurious feel of fresh cotton or linen sheets, which also absorb moisture and let your skin 'breathe' in a way that synthetics never can. Since natural fibres take dye more readily, too, any colours you choose will be deeper and longer lasting. At one time, cotton/synthetic blends were the only choice if you wanted an easy-care finish, but modern technology can now give pure cotton the same quality.

Sadly, pure linen is very costly (although it lasts for generations and its texture improves with age), and it is sold through comparatively few outlets. Cotton, however, is much more widely available in one or more of its many versions: plain woven cotton (the finest and smoothest is called 'percale'); flannelette, a cosy, brushed cotton with strong nursery appeal; crisp, textured piqué, or even cotton jersey, which has the tactile softness of a favourite T-shirt.

Modern bedlinen is available in such a vast array of exciting and varied colours and patterns that resourceful decorators often use sheets as curtains, tablecloths or temporary covers for sofas and chairs. When it comes to the bed, however, many classicists (even modern classicists) would claim that

This page: Piled high with stylish cushions and textured throws, this expansive double bed provides a welcoming corner for relaxation at any time of day. To maximize limited floor space, tuck your bed in a corner.

Opposite: In a duvet-dominated world, many people still prefer to sleep under woollen blankets and a separate top sheet.

white (or natural, undyed) bedlinen is the truly stylish option – a subtle border of lace, drawn-thread work or self-coloured embroidery constituting the only appropriate adornment. On a practical level, there is something to be said for this point of view: white sheets, pillowcases and duvet covers all go together beautifully. They are also easy to maintain (you can wash them at high temperatures and use bleach if necessary), they won't fade and they never date. If you find the lure of funky patterns and pure, vivid colours too strong to resist, however, try to choose all the items you need from the same, or at least coordinating, ranges. That way if, over time, things get lost or damaged, the other pieces in the set can still be used.

Duvets do not usually have a bedspread on top, but if you want one, choose something with a little bit of weight to ensure a smooth surface: a thin quilt is ideal. If your bed is made up with a blanket and top sheet, protect them with a simple, purpose-made cover or improvise by draping the bed with soft throws, silky shawls or exotic sari lengths.

This page: Pure white cotton has a fresh, contemporary look even when it's adorned with traditional tucks, gathers and self-coloured embroidery.

Opposite: The surface of a double bed takes up a considerable proportion of the space in a small room. Here, an extravagantly tufted cover reinforces the quirky colour theme and adds textural interest.

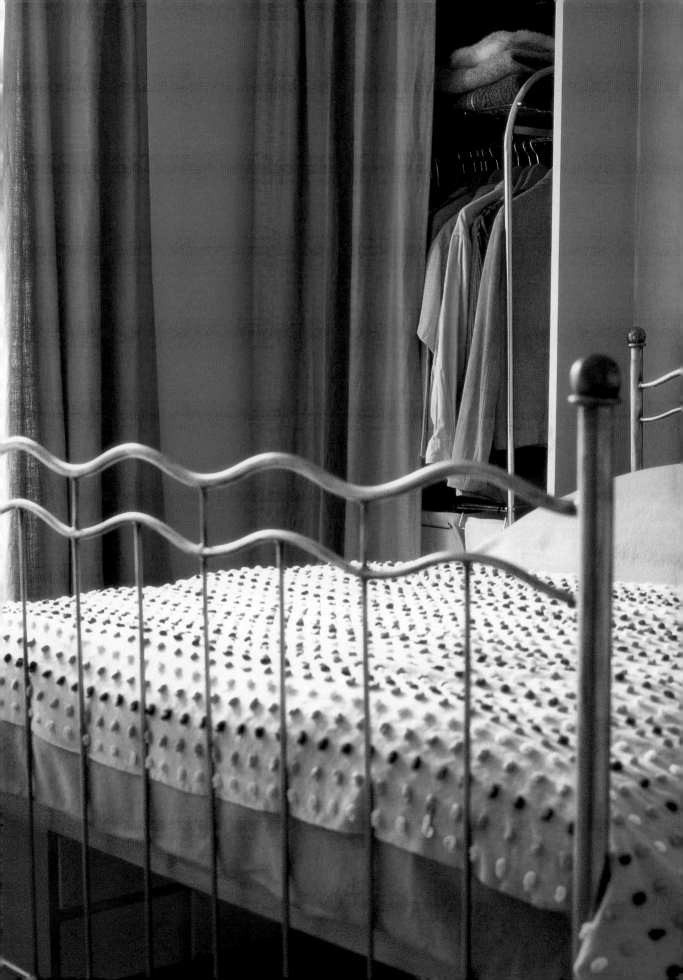

STORAGE &
OTHER FURNITURE

Because of the potential scope and complexity of bedroom storage requirements, it's particularly useful to work out exactly what you intend to store here. In addition to your clothing and accessories, what about extra bedlinen, sports equipment and luggage? The fact that so many disparate and personal possessions are housed in this private sanctuary makes it very easy for insidiously creeping clutter to invade every corner. Without the incentive of tidying up for guests, a carelessly draped sweater, a few pairs of shoes, a pile of ironing and a jumble of grooming products can suddenly turn a cool, stylish room into a domestic disaster area.

In some cases, your first line of defence might be a slight change of tactic: could you adapt another space to accommodate some of these items? If you have a small box room, install built-in units, or a neat system of deep shelves and hanging rails that covers one whole wall; hide it behind a full-length curtain that pulls to one side to afford access.

Even if you don't want a fitted storage system, a freestanding wardrobe or hanging rail, a chest of drawers, a trunk or just a stack of stylish storage boxes located elsewhere could relieve a great deal of pressure on your bedroom. If you don't have a spare room, a wide landing or a space underneath the stairs may be big enough for a piece of supplementary storage furniture.

When the climate you live in has wide seasonal variations, you'll not only make better use of space but also save yourself a lot of trouble if you separate your wardrobe into winter and summer clothes. Twice a year, bring out the ones you'll need for the approaching season, and stash the others neatly away. (Try a box specially shaped to fit under the bed; some of these are made in clear plastic so you can see instantly what's inside, and a few are on castors for ease of access. If you don't need under-bed storage boxes for clothing, they're also ideal for holding spare blankets and

pillows, sports equipment and Christmas decorations.) At a stroke, you'll halve your storage needs, make it easier to find things, and prevent much of the creasing that results when you cram too many garments into a limited space.

hanging space

One of the biggest headaches you're likely to face is taking on a bedroom with no integral storage facilities – a period property, say, or a newer one converted from commercial use. Your options here are choosing individual items of furniture, or installing a built-in system. The classic, low-cost way of providing hanging space is in the form of a clothing rail fitted on castors, perhaps hidden behind a folding screen, or draped with a giant cover to keep off dust and strong sunlight. If your budget allows, choose a new wardrobe from one of the many ranges on the market, or take the techno-chic route and hang your clothes in a classic metal locker; reinforce the look by storing foldables such as underwear and sweaters in a tall filing cabinet, and use one or two smaller ones with an appropriate arrangement of drawers as bedside tables. If you respond to the charm of period furniture, try to find a pretty antique wardrobe and chest of drawers, or explore junk shops and markets for cheap ones that you can restore or revamp.

If you like the idea of a fitted system, choose a purpose-designed storage range from a specialist supplier, or decide what you want and commission a local joiner to make it for you. When there are deep alcoves somewhere in the room, one popular tactic is to turn them into semi-fitted cupboards by putting in shelves and hanging rails, and adding doors on the front. Alternatively, go for a more unusual (and cheaper) form of camouflage such as exotic curtains or a large blind.

Fitted or freestanding, your hanging space will work much harder for you if it's properly organized. For example, a huge amount of valuable space is often wasted when you hang clothes of different lengths together in a mindless jumble: after all, a jacket or a pair of folded trousers is much shorter than a coat or a long dress. Take the trouble to re-arrange your clothes so that garments of one kind, such as shirts, are together and beside items of a similar length. It may then be possible to expand your hanging space by fixing a half-height rail below the original one.

Above: Hanging short garments together creates enough room for an extra rail, a shoe rack or a pile of boxes.

Opposite: Clever shoe freaks label each box with a snapshot of its contents.

Basket drawers on runners are
neatly stacked in freestanding units
mounted on castors.

If you don't have a full-length mirror elsewhere, try incorporating one into your hanging space, on the back of a door, maybe. Otherwise, find a long mirror with an attractive frame or a nicely bevelled edge, and fix it to the wall.

smaller items & accessories

Things like underwear, nightclothes, sweaters and T-shirts should be tidied away out of sight and protected from dust. The system you choose for storing them, however, should allow you to see clearly what's there, and extract what you want without disturbing everything else. Immaculately folded items piled high on open shelves, therefore, are not a good idea. Some organizing systems include clear boxes or pretty, shallow baskets for socks or bras. If this idea appeals to you, copy it in your own hanging space or shelving system. Most people, however, find it more convenient to store small and folded garments in drawers: deep ones for bulky clothing like heavy knitwear and miscellanea such as a mending kit, and shallow ones for smaller items. (Or, if you're very short of space, think about commissioning a bespoke timber bed base that is high enough for a set of drawers to be incorporated underneath – maybe with integral steps for access.)

Baskets and drawers are also useful for holding accessories such as belts, scarves, ties and gloves. Many of these, though, are easier to get at when you hang them on a row of hooks – concealed on the back of a cupboard door, or creating a colourful design feature on the wall, along with your favourite necklaces and bracelets, decorative bags and hats. If display sounds a more appealing option than concealment, set off your collection and give it a professional, finished look by investing in a length of Shaker peg rail. As well as hooks, think about putting up a colourful wall pocket made from rigid plastic or bright fabric, which will swallow up everything from grooming products in various tubes and bottles to rolled-up magazines and a hair dryer.

Right: An inexpensive drawer tidy will eliminate your daily search for the right jewellery or make-up (above). Store frequently worn shoes in a multi-tiered rack to keep them neat and easily accessible (below).

tables & chairs

At its most basic, your bedside table should have a surface large enough to accommodate things like a reading lamp, a selection of books and magazines, a water glass, tissues, telephone and so forth. It's a shame, though, to waste the space underneath, so if you haven't chosen a small chest or trunk to fulfil this function, try to find a piece of furniture that has one or more fitted shelves, or a single drawer at least.

When your main grooming area is in the bathroom, you can do without a work-height table, although if there's no suitable surface in the living room, a quiet corner in the bedroom for letter writing is always an appealing prospect. If you like the idea of a dressing table here, however, (always worth considering to alleviate the inevitable pressure two busy people will put on a tiny bathroom first thing in the morning), there are plenty of style options beside kidney-shaped monstrosities with frilly skirts. A small desk, dining or kitchen table, for example, would be just the right height, and you could use the existing drawers (or add a separate drawer pedestal) to hide away bottles, jars, brushes and bits of cotton wool, which so effectively lower the tone of even the most expensively decorated room. To equip the surface for its new function, place a freestanding mirror on top, or fix an extendable magnifying mirror to the nearest wall. If possible, position your dressing table so that when you're sitting at it, daylight illuminates your face directly. For night-time use, add a simple table lamp (with a bulb of at least 60 watts) whose beam is similarly directed toward your face rather than the mirror.

One particularly effective tactic is to plan a surface like this as a multi-functional work space: keep toiletries and grooming equipment in one drawer (or a covered box or basket) and stationery, stamps and writing implements in another. Choose an adjustable task lamp, which can be swivelled toward your face or your writing surface, and is ideal for illuminating either one. Since neither activity is likely to involve long hours of application, there's no need to provide a sophisticated and expensive task chair, but one with some padding – at least on the seat – is infinitely preferable to a hard wooden, plastic or metal chair, which – no matter how groovy it looks – will become intolerably uncomfortable after an alarmingly short time.

A small, upholstered occasional chair looks inviting in the bedroom, offers a change of shape and proportion from bulky, squarish items such as the bed and the wardrobe, and provides a useful surface on which to set out garments for consideration, or fling them heedlessly at the end of the day. If this is the only role such a chair will play, cover it with almost any fabric that catches your fancy. However, if this chair is also intended to furnish a peaceful corner for reading or contemplation, take care to choose a cover that will withstand the kind of wear this role entails.

Above: A classic cane armchair is comfortable and easy to move from place to place.

Top: This solid wooden chest provides an additional display surface and plenty of extra concealed storage space too.

Designed in 1969 by
Anna Castelli Ferrieri,
this classic storage system
consists of individual plastic
cylinders and a separate tray
top. These basic elements
can be combined to create a
unit of whatever height or
capacity you require: stack two
or three to make a bedside
table, or add more for a modern
take on the traditional tallboy.

8 bathrooms

Of all the design challenges you face, your bathroom is often the most challenging, as well as the most rewarding: challenging because there are so many practical needs to be met in what is notoriously the smallest room, and rewarding because this space responds so dramatically to basic design tactics such as changing the colour

scheme, or adding an imaginative window treatment. Begin by getting to grips with the basic services and sanitary fittings involved (which technological advances have made cheaper in real terms than they were 20 years ago), then enjoy creating your own private cocoon of fantasy and indulgence that will make you feel pampered, relaxed and refreshed whenever you emerge.

This page: Special scaled-down corner fittings (basin, cistern and shower unit) allow an en-suite bathroom to be squeezed into one corner of a large master bedroom.

Opposite: Ambient light from a recessed spot washes over a bathroom wall clad in two very different types of ceramic tile.

PLANNING

If you are remodelling your bathroom completely, or creating a bathroom where there wasn't one before, you have a chance to plan the room from scratch. Step one, as always, is to decide which fittings, accessories and extras you want. The minimum requirement is a bath (and/or shower), a basin, a toilet, a mirror and storage of some kind. If you have enough floor space, consider installing a bidet, a second basin (useful, if two of you need to wash at the same time) or a separate shower. Or free up space in the kitchen by siting the washing machine here; the plumbing, after all, will already be in place. When a bathroom has been converted from a bedroom (common in period properties), it's often big enough to cope with much more than the standard suite.

practical floor plans

Small bathrooms, too, can accommodate a surprising amount if you choose a range of scaled-down sanitaryware; some also include ingenious corner cisterns and basins, and even storage cabinets. As well as small-space fittings, explore those that increase the impression of space by being wall fixed rather than floor standing. Fitted bathrooms, which resemble fitted kitchens in that the elements are linked by matching built-in units, provide a generous expanse of worktop and ample storage capacity. While these systems do minimize visual and actual clutter in a small bathroom, they seldom suit the limited proportions of the space, and can look bulky and dated; as a result, they have never really caught on.

When you're revamping an existing bathroom, the job will be cheaper and less complex if you can maintain the existing positions of the water and waste pipes and the soil stack (the latter is the trickiest to move). This doesn't necessarily mean the fittings have to go in the same place, though: the bath could run along a different wall, as long as the taps don't wander too far from their original position. To make the most of your space, for example, choose a shorter bath that will fit across the width of the room rather than running along its length. Even if it stays in exactly the same place, a shorter bath might allow you to fit a deep shelf for bottles, jars and scented candles at one end, and as an ecologically sound

bonus, it will take much less water to fill. Or position the basin and toilet side by side, boxing in the pipework for both of them behind a false wall topped with a useful shelf. When the original layout is markedly wasteful of space and awkward to use, the cost and upheaval involved in moving pipework is likely to be justified.

When you're drawing up your plans, bear in mind that each fitting needs a minimum amount of clearance to be used comfortably. Allow 1,100 x 700 mm (43 x 28 in) beside a bath; 200 mm (8 in) either side and 700 mm (28 in) in front of a basin; 200 mm (8 in) either side and 600 mm (24 in) in front of a toilet or bidet. For showers enclosed on three sides, allow 900 x 700 mm (35 x 28 in), and for unenclosed showers 900 x 400 mm (35 x 16 in). This may seem like an enormous amount of space, but as only one (at most two) fittings are likely to be used at the same time, the clearance areas can — and should — overlap.

lighting

In terms of lighting, bathrooms have exactly the same needs as any other room: strong task lighting and soft, ambient illumination. To guarantee a clear view of face and hair, install tungsten lamps near the mirror directed not at the reflective surface, but at the person in front of it. The traditional dressing-table arrangement beloved of Hollywood films is ideal, but fittings on either side, or even a single one above, will do. If these lights are wired to a dimmer switch, you can turn them down to a subtle glow when you want a relaxing bath. Otherwise, recessed spots or a similarly gentle ceiling fitting will produce appropriate background illumination.

surfaces & schemes

The materials you choose for your bathroom should be resistant not only to water, but also to steam and condensation. Here, the floor won't get as much wear as the one in the kitchen, but it's more likely to get drenched, so it should be completely impervious as well as easy to clean and non-slip, even when it's wet. (One advantage of a small bathroom, though, is that you can often afford really luxurious flooring since you need so little of it.) Hard floors (like those made from stone or ceramic tile) are certainly durable and waterproof, but they're also cold and some are slippery. Neither wood nor laminate will emerge unscathed from constant soaking, but bamboo flooring (which has a similar look) is more water resistant. Other wise choices are vinyl, linoleum and rubber flooring, which are all soft and warm to walk on, non-slip and waterproof. The surface of rubber flooring, however, does not respond well to bleach, so if you are particularly addicted to its use in the bathroom, choose something else instead.

Moisture can also affect fabrics, so if the room is damp, choose blinds or shutters in preference to curtains. At best, damp will leave them limp and bedraggled; at worst it will cause mildew. One alternative might be to use shower curtains (shortened, if necessary) at the window. Or eschew any form of window treatment and replace the clear glass with mirror glass. If the basin is under the window, it can do double duty as a grooming mirror.

The most vulnerable areas of wall – around the bath, the basin and the shower (if any) – should be well protected, and the most popular way to do this is with ceramic tiles. Here, as in the kitchen, white ones are the least expensive. They are perennially stylish, will complement any style and are more likely to appeal to potential buyers when you want to sell. If these factors lose out to a lust for colour and pattern, visit a specialist shop to check out the enormous range of wall tiles available: plain and adorned with hand painting, printed patterns and surreal photo images.

If you inherit stained or ugly tiles, replacing them is the best option. If that's not possible, then try disguising them with a special tile paint: the result will not duplicate the finish or durability of new tiles (and will not be suitable for a shower cubicle), but it will look better than what's there. Or, if you can live with the tiles but not their grubby grouting, freshen it up with white paint (instructions in most DIY manuals), or look out for a proprietary cleaning solution.

Around a shower, the wallcovering has to be a completely waterproof one like tiles or glass. For the splashback area behind the basin and the bath, however, you can choose from a much wider range of materials.

For the main areas of walls and ceiling, paint is the easiest and most rewarding material to use and provides the most practical finish. Try one of the ranges specially designed for bathrooms, or standard vinyl silk, which has a wipe-down finish. The similarly soft sheen of eggshell paint looks better on woodwork than hard, shiny gloss, and is less likely to attract beads of condensation. When your bathroom is free from damp (more likely if it's used by only one or two people rather than a large family), there's no reason why you can't hang wallpaper – just use a special fungicidal adhesive.

If your design preferences run to the cool and sparse, keep your palette simple and subtle. Because this space tends to be occupied for limited periods only, however, it can also take vibrant hues and novelty themes that would be overpowering elsewhere. So, if you've always longed for a seaside scheme with stripy beach-hut cladding, rope accessories and piles of shells, or a fantasy garden with trompe l'oeil pergolas, lush greenery and classical columns, this is the place to create it.

Above: Colour-matched tiles and timber cladding surround this period bath.

Opposite: Here, pale painted walls are protected with sheets of sandblasted glass. Echoing its natural look are a beech bath panel and limestone flooring.

FITTINGS

One of the first things that many people do when they take on a new home is to rip out the existing bathroom suite and replace it with something they've chosen themselves. The majority go for new fittings, but if you like the idea of authentic old ones, explore your local architectural salvage yard.

Of all the bathroom fittings purchased each year, by far the biggest proportion are white, and for all the usual reasons: it has a fresh, clean look; it's easy to care for; it always looks stylish, and it never inspires the disdain in potential buyers that flamingo pink or harvest gold almost guarantee. Another smart, but very costly option is stainless steel. Although fittings in this material have only recently become fashionable in the domestic market, they are common in public buildings because they are virtually indestructible.

Modern bathroom manufacturers produce ranges in a stunning array of styles. Among these, you'll find two main types of design for what is known as sanitaryware: basins, toilets and bidets – floorstanding and wall-hung. Some companies offer ranges in both versions. Floorstanding fittings are the most popular since they tend to be least expensive and simplest to install, but wall-hung designs have many advantages: they can be fixed at any height so they're ideal for tall people and those with limited mobility, and they leave the floor completely clear, which not only makes cleaning easier, but also increases the apparent size of the room.

baths

There are three main types of domestic bath:

- **Plastic baths** (acrylic, fibreglass or fibreglass-reinforced acrylic) are the cheapest, the lightest, the easiest to mould into complex shapes and the simplest to install. Made of either sheet or cast material (cast plastic is thicker and more expensive), they are also the least durable and the most prone to surface damage. Some lesser-quality models can also shift unsettlingly when you get in and out.
- **Enamelled pressed steel baths** are a practical, mid-range choice. Slightly more expensive than plastic, enamelled steel is hardwearing, good-looking and easy to look after.

- **Enamelled cast iron baths** are the most expensive and the heaviest; few floors above ground level are strong enough to support them, especially when they're full. They are usually large, and swallow up plenty of hot water. Cast iron is an excellent conductor of heat, though, so even a full bath cools down quickly. Most old baths you see in salvage yards are made of cast iron, their chips and cracks bearing witness to the vulnerability of its surface. Modern manufacturers make these baths in contemporary shapes and reproduction styles with claw feet and roll-top edges.

A few specialist firms also make baths in thick glass, marine timber, copper and solid marble, but these are prohibitively expensive. Most baths are rectangular, but you can also find round, oval and keyhole shapes. Deep, square baths with a seat (called 'sitz baths' or 'shower tub baths') come into their own when logic tells you to replace your bath with a shower for space reasons, but you don't want to give up the luxury of a long soak. Also popular for pampering and relaxation are whirlpool and spa baths, which provide different forms of hydro massage. Both types are more effective when they come as a complete unit, as opposed to hardware that undertakes to adapt an existing bath.

- **Whirlpools** combine water with air bubbles, then force it into the bath through jets in the side.
- **Spas** soothe and relax you by blowing gentle air bubbles into the water through holes in the base of the bath.

This page: Spanning a modestly proportioned room exactly, this plain white bath has plenty of room inside, yet takes full advantage of available space. Note the efficient use of surrounding wall space for storage.

Below left: Cast iron baths can be re-enamelled, but this is a costly and inconvenient job, since it has to be done in a specialist workshop. Some types of resurfacing are done in situ, but the result is not permanent.

showers

There are also three main types of shower:

- **Instantaneous electric showers** are the cheapest and the easiest to install. They heat the water as it passes through, so the temperature of your shower can vary with that of the incoming supply. This type of shower is the least satisfactory since it can produce a weak and unreliable flow.
- **Mixer showers** combine hot and cold water in a central valve. For reasons of water pressure, this system is suitable only where hot water is stored in a tank, rather than heated as it's used. If the tank is less than 100 mm (39 in) above the shower, you'll need a pump to increase the flow.
- **Power showers** have an integral pump, so they provide a reliably strong and adjustable flow. Not surprisingly, they also use more water than other types of shower and they are the most complex to install and expensive to buy.

Most showers have an adjustable head so you can choose between needle-sharp jets of water, a concentrated stream or a bubbly flow. Showers can be fitted over a bath or in a separate cubicle (built-in or freestanding) with a tray at the bottom (ceramic or plastic). Extremely appealing, but of limited application, is the idea of a walk-in shower (or wet room); a dedicated chamber with a large, high shower head, fully tiled surfaces and a drain in the floor.

basins

Almost all bathroom basins are made of glazed vitreous china; a few come in materials more usually associated with kitchens, like stainless steel or Corian, and the odd sculptural design is produced in ribbed glass or marine timber. Again, there are three main styles:

- **Pedestal basins** are the most common type and often the cheapest. They sit on ceramic columns that conceal the pipework and help to support the bowl, which is also screwed to the wall with brackets. Their main drawback is their fixed height, which is too low for many adults to use comfortably. (To test yours, stand with your arms straight down in front of you and your hands at right angles, palms down. If your palms aren't touching the bottom of the basin, it's too low.)
- **Wall-hung basins**, which are supported solely by concealed brackets, can be fixed at any height. The pipes are hidden behind a neat, ceramic cover or left exposed. If you take the latter option, ask your plumber to replace the ugly, plastic waste outlet with a shiny, metal one called a 'bottle trap'.
- **Inset basins** are like kitchen sinks; they fit into a larger work surface or vanity unit and are fixed in the same way (see pages 146–7 and 144–5 for sections on

Above: In this blindingly white bathroom, an unusual hoop-shaped curtain rail tops the large, deep shower tray, built-in and tiled to match the walls and floor.

Above right: Install a super-shiny shower head made from chrome-plated brass.

worktops and sinks). Semi-inset basins slot into a half-depth surface so the pipework is hidden, while the front of the basin breaks the edge with its curve.

Bathroom basins come in a range of sizes, from those that are as big as kitchen sinks to miniature cloackroom designs. When your bathroom is tiny, try using a cloakroom basin instead of a conventional size; if you need it only for washing your hands and face, this solution would work well.

Left: This unusual ceramic basin was clearly inspired by those found in farmhouse kitchens.

Below left: With its 1930s ocean-liner styling, this pedestal basin cries out for a porthole-shaped mirror.

Below: If your budget is bigger than your bathroom, choose a compact integral basin and cupboard in stainless steel.

taps

Baths and basins are usually available with whatever arrangement of holes is required for the taps you choose, or with no holes at all so you can choose fittings that are plumbed directly into the wall, leaving the rim completely clear. (Some baths are designed so the taps can go at either end or in the middle, doing away with a 'tap' end altogether.)

For both baths and basins, you can choose between separate HOT and COLD pillar taps, or more popular and convenient mixer taps, which have either separate HOT and COLD handles or levers, or a single lever that turns and angles to control both the pressure of the water and the temperature. In addition, bath mixers often have a diverter for the shower and a hand-held shower attachment.

Whatever style of taps you choose, make sure you can turn them easily. For sheer user-friendliness, it's hard to beat the traditional cross-head shape, while few examples of domestic design are as ill-suited to their function as handles in the form of smooth spheres or cylinders that are virtually impossible to grip with wet, soapy hands.

Above: Simple chrome shower controls suit the swimming-pool look established by wide expanses of watery mosaic tiles.

Top left: Classic cross-head taps are easy to grip, and they'll never look dated or out of place.

Left: Although it was moulded in one piece, this wall-hung basin conceals its plumbing behind a semi-inset shape.

toilets & bidets

Whatever their design, toilets and bidets are generally made from vitreous china, although some are available in stainless steel too. When you have both fittings, it makes plumbing sense to put them side by side.

There are three basic styles of installation for a toilet:

- **Standard** fittings have a separate cistern and pan linked by a length of pipe. Old-fashioned toilets had very high cisterns, and this option still works in a small space since it allows the pan to sit against the wall. With most modern toilets, however, the cistern is directly above the pan.
- **Close-coupled or one-piece** models resemble a single unit with their streamlined connection between cistern and pan. They look neater than standard toilets and they are easier to clean, but also more expensive.
- **Back-to-wall** toilets have their cistern and plumbing completely concealed behind a full or half-height false wall. Wall-hung models are fitted this way.

In addition to the way they're installed, toilets also differ in the way they flush. On the whole, modern toilets are designed to conserve water, and most use less than those made even a decade ago.

- **Washdown** models are the cheaper, smaller and noisier of the two types on offer. They rely solely on the force and volume of the water flowing into the bowl to clear it.
- **Siphonic** models use suction or compressed air as well as water to clear the bowl, which makes them quieter and more efficient. This type tends to be more expensive, however, and slightly bulkier.

Bidets, too, come in two main types:

- **Over-rim** models are the simplest and cheapest. Like big, low basins, they fill from pillar or mixer taps and empty through a waste outlet in exactly the same way.
- **Below-rim** models fill with warmed water that flows into the bowl around the rim in the form of a flush.

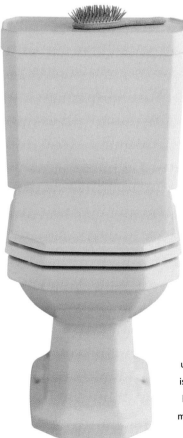

Left: Close-coupled toilets have a neat, unfussy look that, in terms of streamlining, is the next best thing to wall-hung designs. Push the boat out with a top-of-the-range model in stainless steel (far left), or choose subtle Art Deco angles instead (left).

STORAGE & ACCESSORIES

Providing stylish and well-planned storage is a vital part of creating a bathroom that you will enjoy using. As well as articles in current use (like towels, toothbrush, grooming equipment and cosmetics), the items most likely to need a home here are stocks of clean linen, medicines, spare toiletries and toilet rolls (white), cleaning paraphernalia and dirty laundry.

When you have a roomy cupboard or chest elsewhere (in the bedroom or hall, perhaps) you may not have to find room for bulky things like piles of fresh towels. If they do have to go here, try to squeeze in a cupboard, chest of drawers, shelf unit or trolley to accommodate them. Or, when a shower-free bath spans one end of a tiny room, use the space above it for a single, high-level shelf, which will hold not only towels, but toilet rolls, medicine, and seldom-used creams and potions. Suspend it from the top to give an unbroken line underneath, and finish it with a timber strip fixed flush with the bottom edge, which will keep the contents in place; you can also hang clothes from it to dry over the bath.

Floor space allowing, choose a capacious laundry hamper (purpose-designed or improvised from a shiny rubbish bin, or a log basket). Otherwise, hang a laundry bag on a sturdy hook. If there's no storage hole under the basin for cleaners, bleach, sponges, etc., create one by attaching a removable skirt around the edge with Velcro, or keep them in a basket tucked into a corner. Most bathroom manufacturers also supply accessories like cabinets, mirrors, shelves, bath racks, towel rings and rails and holders for soap, glass, toothbrushes, toilet roll and toilet brush. Certainly, a mirrored cabinet above the basin (or a mirror fixed to the wall and a cabinet elsewhere) is extremely useful. These items don't have to match, though, and the rest are optional extras: leave soap on the basin (liquid soap in a pump dispenser won't make a slimy mess), and pile toilet rolls in a basket. A single shelf to hold your toothbrush, razor, glass and comb is much neater than a collection of separate holders.

Fix straight towel rails in preference to rings, which keep damp fabric bunched up so it can't dry properly. If a radiator is taking up valuable floor space, swap it for a combination radiator/heated towel rail that you can attach higher up the wall. Actually, the design and quality of the towels is more important to the overall look and comfort of your bathroom than matching accessories. Choose loopy, cotton towels rather than velvety ones, which are less absorbent. Invest in bath sheets, bath towels for your hair, hand towels, face cloths and cotton bath mats, which are much nicer to stand on when you step out of the bath or shower than rubber or cork mats or wooden slats. An assortment of different-coloured linen looks messy, so buy everything in a single shade, or a limited array of colours that look good in any combination.

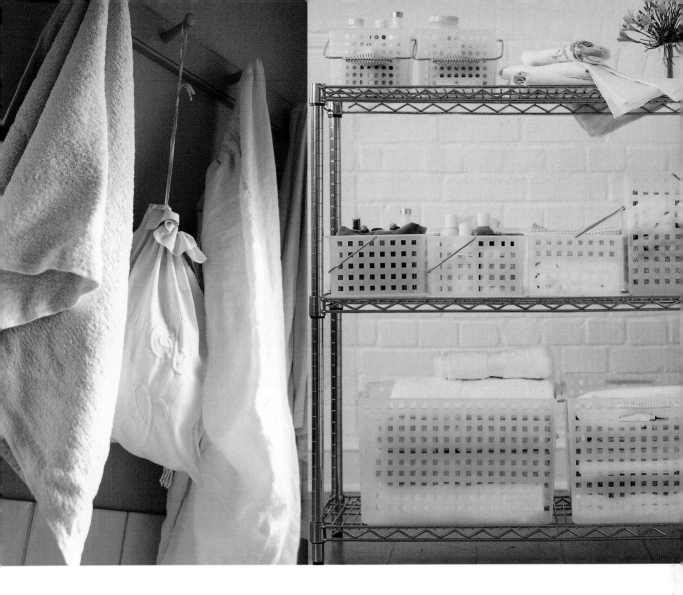

Above: As well as towels and face cloths, a row of hooks will hold big bags for dirty laundry and small ones full of soap, bath preparations, shampoo and cleaning supplies.

Left: Some heated towel rails run off the central heating system, so they only work when the radiators are on. To guarantee warm, dry towels all year round, look for one with a separate electric element as well.

Above right and right: When you rely on open shelves for storage, invest in coordinated boxes and baskets to maintain order. These smart translucent containers come in lots of useful sizes.

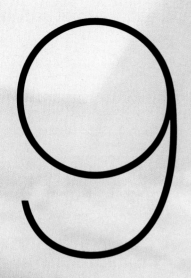

When your head is full of ideas and inspiration, it's easy to lose sight of the areas that connect all your rooms to each other, and to the front door – the entrance hall, stairs, corridors and landings. In many buildings, these spaces

connecting
areas

see more traffic than any single room, and one of them – the hall – will provide many of your visitors with their influential first impression of you and your home. What's almost more important, though, is the fact that the visual and emotional atmosphere you create here will be the first thing to greet you every time you turn the key in the lock and step into your own home.

THE SPACES

The entrance hall, stairs, corridors and landings in most homes are true Cinderella spaces: overworked and over-looked, yet absolutely central to the stylistic and functional success of the overall scheme. Give them the attention they deserve by choosing a single decorative treatment to link them together; one that works well with the looks you've chosen in each of your rooms, so that passing from one area to another doesn't involve any jarring contrasts. Stairways and corridors especially are notorious for their absence of natural light, so aim for gentle, glowing warmth rather than the drama of a deep shade, an exotic pattern or a dizzying mix of textures and materials. Reinforce the subtle, appealing atmosphere you create by fitting simple wall lights or clip-on or recessed spots, and wiring them to a dimmer switch so you can vary their brightness according to the time of day and the amount of sunlight available.

Since these floors will have to withstand heavy and concentrated traffic, it's important to invest in a durable floor covering. However attracted you are to the charms of hardwood strips or bare boards, however, top-quality carpet is a wiser choice, not only because of the way it looks, but also because it insulates well in spaces famous for being draughty, and it also muffles noise – a quality that is sorely needed in connecting areas, especially stairs, where a single pair of running feet can sound like an invading army. Carpet is also safer, since timber floors can be treacherous when they get wet, which they will when you come in after being caught in a downpour, or accidentally spill a drink on your way from the kitchen.

The walls of your linking areas, too, will lead a hard life since anything you bring through the front door, from weekly food shopping to bulky items of furniture, will travel along one or another of them before it reaches its final destination, and there are often a few knocks along the way. A wipeable paint finish, perhaps with a panelled tongue-and-groove section below dado height for extra protection, works well, but be careful of vulnerable surfaces like wallpaper, which not only cost more initially, but also damage easily if they're knocked, and can prove tedious and costly to replace, especially in a lofty stairwell.

Check out all your connecting areas to see if any of them can be encouraged to work a little harder, either by accommodating small items of furniture or built-in shelves, or even by providing space for an extra mini-room: a cloakroom under the stairs, maybe, or a boxed-in tumble dryer on the landing.

Left: Converted industrial spaces suit tough materials and hard-edged shapes that would jar in most purpose-built homes. Here, the satiny sheen of the ladder-like metal stairs is echoed by a slim finishing strip that replaces conventional skirting board.

Opposite: The uncompromising austerity of a truly minimalist scheme requires almost as much discipline to live in as it does to create. Here, dog-leg timber stairs, skylit from above, are unrelieved by any softening texture or colour.

entrance halls

If the front door is solid (without a glass panel) and the windows around it are small (or non-existent), your entrance hall may feel gloomy and claustrophobic. One way of tackling this is to get rid of as many internal doors as possible that lead off it. Doors that lead to the living or dining room, for instance, may hardly ever be used, and removing them – especially if they open out into the hall rather than into the room itself – would give you more space as well as more light.

In practical terms, the most pressing need here is for somewhere to hang outer clothing like coats, hats, scarves and gloves, plus bags, boots and umbrellas (your own and those of your guests) so they don't impose a further storage burden on the bedroom. In the absence of a fitted cupboard, provide a decorative hatstand or a row of hooks on the wall, and perhaps a mirror for last-minute grooming checks. Extremely useful, too, is a shelf big enough to hold keys, post, gloves, briefcase and items you intend to take with you when you next leave the house. If there's any useable floor space, you might be able to fit in a surface of some kind on which you can dump excess baggage as you come in: a chair, for instance, an old pew or a bench, perhaps with a storage compartment underneath for out-of-season footwear.

At its most sophisticated, the concept of equipping your entrance hall with purpose-designed storage can stem the tide of incoming clutter before it overwhelms all your rooms. This could involve tactics like putting up a row of small hooks for your own and your neighbours' keys so you don't have to ransack countless drawers when somebody gets locked out. Similarly, provide a mini-filing system so incoming post can be sorted immediately into letters, bills, catalogues and junk mail that can go straight into a nearby recycling bag without ever sullying the tidiness of your living room.

Some properties – usually older ones – have entrance halls as big as small rooms, and these can sometimes be exploited as occasional dining, working or letter-writing areas. If there isn't room for a small table, perhaps you could install a flap-down surface hinged to the wall so it can disappear when it's no longer needed.

However tough your floor covering, it's a good idea to give it some extra help right inside the entrance. As well as a waterproof mat near the coat rack on which you can dump wet shoes, boots and umbrellas, put down a large doormat or even an inexpensive runner, on which any surface grime you bring in from outside can be dispersed before it gets tracked into every room.

If chilling draughts tend to creep in around your front door (and especially if you use your entrance hall periodically as a living space), take the trouble to fix a proprietary flap over your letter box, and strips of insulation around the frame. For the ultimate in efficient, time-honoured and decorative draught-proofing, hang a thick, soft door curtain that you can pull across when necessary to block off the entrance completely.

Right: Recessed spotlights set into the riser ensure that the change of level in this hallway doesn't trip up the unwary.

Opposite: This spacious entrance hall has many features worth copying: a bench, a shelf and lots of useful hooks.

stairs

More than any other connecting area – and even more than most rooms – the design of your stairs should be undertaken with a strict regard for safety: a slippery tread or a loose nail could cause a serious accident, so unless you have decided on something quirky like studded rubber or tread-plate aluminium, it's advisable to carpet your stairs rather than leaving them with a hard surface like bare or painted timber.

The suitability of conventional carpet for use on stairs will depend on the density and type of its weave, so before you make your final choice, check this information with your supplier. When natural floor coverings like sisal and coir first appeared in the domestic marketplace, the majority were too loosely woven and unstable for this purpose. Most modern weaves, though (with the exception of a few with deep-relief patterns), perform just as well here as carpet. Where they do differ, however, is in their dependence on skilful, experienced fitting. If they're not stapled tightly around the contour of each stair, they can work loose and present a safety hazard.

Stair carpet of all descriptions can be either closely fitted or laid in the form of a runner (plain, or with a woven border) that covers only the central section. Runners are sometimes cheaper and they appeal to those who like to see a flash of floorboard, but they do draw in the eye and make the whole stairway look narrower than if it were closely carpeted.

When carpeting your stairway is still some distance down your list of financial priorities (or if your heart is set on floorboards), improve their appearance with a proprietary floor paint. If your stairs are in constant use, paint alternate treads, then let them dry completely so you can step on them when you paint the rest.

Take ·advantage of the expanse of wall that adjoins your stairs by using it as a themed display area for family photographs, political cartoons or even favourite magazine covers. Avoid the temptation, though, to echo the line of the stairs by hanging your pictures in a stepped formation running from top to bottom. Instead, arrange them in several separate groups spaced out along the length of the stairway.

This page: Timber takes all the leading roles in these elegant connecting areas: near the entrance as a dark and polished shelf, on the stairway as a glowing mahogany handrail, and throughout in the form of pale floorboards.

Opposite page above: Soft, warm, quiet and safe, traditional stair carpet makes a perfect foil for the bold and steely surfaces that surround it.

Opposite page below: With its non-slip surface and textural variety, tread-plate aluminium is an ideal covering for stairs in constant use.

Finally, pay close attention to the way your stairs are lit. This is one place where a conventional ceiling light (a pendant or a recessed spot) works extremely well, since it creates a sharp contrast between the well-lit treads and the dark risers; make sure the fitting you choose doesn't compromise your vision, though, by producing glare. The illumination you provide here needn't be strong, as long as it allows you to see the stairs clearly. To provide maximum control, wire your overhead light to a two-way switch so you can control it from top and bottom. Or take a sleeker, more sophisticated approach and install tiny, recessed spots set low in the wall or the skirting board beside every other tread.

corridors & landings

Inject personality into the least prepossessing passages by using their walls for display and picking out one or two distinctive items with subtle accent lights that will also act as background illumination.

Explore the potential of any accessible floor space – at the end of a corridor, maybe, or on a wide landing – by trying to find a small table, chair, chest or plant stand that would not only provide precious extra room for storage or display, but also make sure that every corner of your home is indelibly stamped with your own distinctive personality and sense of style.

FURTHER REFERENCE

home-starter basics

When you finally move into your home, it's tempting to neglect the more pedestrian aspects of domestic independence: things like security, insurance and safety, as well as essential services such as electricity and water. If you lead a charmed existence, this all-too-understandable avoidance may have few consequences. If, however, you turn out to be subject to the same accidents, crises and irritating disruptions as the rest of us, dealing with the basics at this stage will help you to cope calmly and effectively.

UTILITIES & SERVICES

As soon as you assume responsibility for your premises, make contact with the companies that supply electricity, gas, water and telecommunications. If the services are not connected, make arrangements to have this done and confirm them in writing. If you are taking over the bills from someone else, let the relevant authority know when this is to happen.

Establish all the essential information: where (and how) the water and the gas can be turned off, for example, the location of the fuse box and what telephone number to use in case of emergencies. Make a note of this data and keep it somewhere safe and easy to find so that if disaster strikes in the form of a burst pipe or a gas leak, you'll know what to do and who to call for help.

Without getting too technical, familiarize yourself with the way your heating system works, how to turn it on and off, when it should be serviced and who to call if it breaks down. Many gas systems, for example, have electric controls, so if there is a problem with either supply, you'll have no heat.

Most utilities provide extensive information, too, about things like energy efficiency, safety and economy, so make full use of any material on offer.

INSURANCE

Essentially, there are two types: building insurance, which covers the actual bricks and mortar (and will therefore not be relevant if you are a tenant), and contents insurance, which covers all your possessions. If you are buying your home, building insurance is not optional – your mortgage provider will insist that you take it out. Contents insurance, in theory, is optional, but trying to save money by doing without it is the ultimate false economy: if you're burgled or your home is damaged by fire or flooding, you could suffer crippling losses. Unless you have reason to use one particular insurer, you may find it easier to go through a broker, who will advise you on the best policy for your needs and your budget.

When it comes to working out the value of your worldly goods, be sure to take everything into consideration; it's easy enough to estimate the price of expensive things like the television, video, computer and appliances, but the combined worth of your CDs, say, plus your clothing and your books is likely to surprise you.

Read your policy carefully and comply with its requirements: you may have to fit special locks to your doors and windows, for instance, or advise your insurers if you plan to work from home, especially if you intend employing other people or accommodating regular visitors. If you do make a claim and it turns out you've ignored the conditions laid down, your insurance will be invalid.

SECURITY

Ensuring that your premises – and the occupants – are secure is a vital part of creating a home. Most local police stations will provide detailed advice on domestic security, and some will even send a specially trained officer to inspect the existing arrangements and let you know how they can be improved. You may sleep more soundly if, as well as strong, suitable locks for doors and windows, you fit an alarm system, a set of security grilles and/or an outside light that switches on automatically when anyone comes near. If you're away frequently, invest in a timer that turns lamps on and off at selected times, making it look as if the rooms are occupied.

However prone you are to locking yourself out, never hide a key in the garden; there's no place an experienced burglar can't find.

SAFETY

The fact that most accidents happen at home is no less relevant for being often repeated, but some of the most efficient precautions are also the simplest.

If you store anything above your reach, make sure you have a sturdy surface to stand on for access: small steps or a strong, steady stool. Take note of things like sharp corners that you continually bump into, or patches of floor where you often stumble or slip, and do something about them before they cause serious injury.

When it comes to fire safety, absorb the received wisdom and act on it: avoid second-hand foam furniture that may ignite easily and give off deadly fumes; never smoke in bed; don't ignore worn cables or flexes, and make sure electrical sockets aren't overloaded. Buy a smoke alarm and replace the battery regularly. There's no need to invest in a fire extinguisher (different types of fire require different models), but if you do a lot of cooking, keep a fire blanket in the kitchen so that if a greasy pan catches alight, you can smother the flames: dousing oil-based fires with water will cause them to flare dramatically with lethal consequences.

further reading

Style

Ashwell, Rachel, *Shabby Chic*, New York, HarperCollins, 1996

Calloway, Stephen, *Baroque: The Culture of Excess*, London, Phaidon, 1994

Hall, Dinah, *Ethnic by Design*, London, Mitchell Beazley, 1992

Hoppen, Kelly, *East Meets West*, London, Conran Octopus, 1997

Miller, Judith and Martin, *Period Style*, London, Mitchell Beazley, 1989

Miller, Judith and Martin, *Country Style*, London, Mitchell Beazley, 1990

Slesin, Suzanne and Cliff, Stafford, *English Style*, London, Thames & Hudson, 1984

Slesin, Suzanne and Cliff, Stafford, *French Style*, London, Thames & Hudson, 1984

Slesin, Suzanne and Cliff, Stafford, *Japanese Style*, London, Thames & Hudson, 1987

Snodin, Michael and Stavenow-Hidemark, Elisabet, *Carl and Karin Larsson: Creators of the Swedish Style*, London, V & A Publications, 1997

Sprigg, June, and Larkin, David, *Shaker: Life, Work, and Art*, London, Seven Dials, Cassell & Co, 2000

Decorating & Furnishing

Boase, Petra, *Funky Junk*, London, Carlton Books, 1999

Conran, Sebastian and Bond, Mark, *Contemporary Lighting*, London, Conran Octopus, 1999

Dixon, Tom, *Rethink*, London, Conran Octopus, 2000

Innes, Jocasta, *The New Paint Magic*, London, Frances Lincoln, 1992

Mack, Lorrie, *Living in Small Spaces*, London, Conran Octopus, 1988

Mack, Lorrie, *Calm Working Spaces*, London, Marshall Publishing, 2000

Robinson, Lynne, and Lowther, Richard, *Decorative Paint Recipes*, London, Quadrille, 1999

Robinson, Lynne and Lowther, Richard, *Windows: Recipes and Ideas*, London, Quadrille, 2000

Smith, Delia, *How to Cook: Book One*, London, BBC Books, 1998

Smith, Delia, *How to Cook: Book Two*, London, BBC Books, 1999 (clear, sound advice on kitchen equipment as well as food)

Tanqueray, Rebecca, *Eco Chic*, London, Carlton Books, 2000

Whitemore, Maureen, *The Home Furnishings Workbook*, London, Collins & Brown, 2000

suppliers

(unless otherwise stated, the following companies all supply general furnishings and accessories)

Aero
347–9 King's Road
London SW3 5ES
tel: 020 7351 0511
enqs.: 020 8971 0066
www.aero-furniture.com

The Amtico Company Ltd
PO Box 42
Kingfield Road
Coventry,
West Midlands CV6 5PL
tel: 01203 864100
fax: 01203 861552
www.amtico.co.uk
(vinyl flooring)

Laura Ashley by Post
FREEPOST, PO Box 5
Newtown
Powys, Wales SY16 1LX
tel: 0800 868 100
fax: 01686 621273
www.lauraashley.com

Astracast plc
PO Box 20
Spring Ram Business Park
Birstall, West Yorks. WF17 9XD
tel: 01924 477466
fax: 01924 351331
colour@astracast.co.uk
www.astracast.co.uk
(kitchen and bathroom fittings)

Bisque Radiators
15 Kingsmead Square
Bath, Avon BA1 2AE
tel: 01225 469244
fax: 01225 444708
(showroom also at 244 Belsize Road, London NW6 4BT)

J W Bollom & Co Ltd
Croydon Road
Beckenham
Kent BR3 4BL
tel: 020 8658 2299
fax: 020 8658 8672
sales@bollom.com
www.bollom.com
(paint, wood finishes and exhibition materials)

Bombay Duck
231 The Vale
London W3 7QS
tel: 020 8749 8001
fax: 020 8749 9000
info@bombayduck.co.uk
http://www.bombay.duck.co.uk

Couverture
310 King's Road
London SW3 5UH
tel: 020 7795 1200
fax: 020 7795 1202
info@couverture.co.uk
(hand-decorated bedlinen and accessories)

Crosslee plc
Lightcliffe Factory
Hipperholme
Halifax, W Yorkshire
HX3 8DE
tel: 01422 203555
fax: 01422 206304
http://www.crosslee.co.uk
(domestic appliances including tumble dryers in bright colours)

Crown Paints
tel: stockists information
01254 704951
www.crownpaint.co.uk
www.sandtex.co.uk
(paints and decorative-effect kits)

Crucial Trading
PO Box 11
Duke Place
Kidderminster
Worcestershire DY10 2JR
tel: 0800 374429
fax: 01562 820030
floors@tomkinsons.co.uk
(natural floor coverings)

Cucina Direct Ltd
PO Box 6611
London SW15 2WG
tel: 0870 727 4300
fax: 0870 727 4330
www.cucinadirect.co.uk
(kitchen equipment and tableware)

Dalsouple Direct Ltd
PO Box 140
Bridgwater
Somerset TA5 1HT
tel: 01984 667551
fax: 01984 618397
info@dalsouple.com
www.dalsouple.com
(rubber flooring)

**The Domestic
Paraphernalia Co.**
Unit 15
Marine Business Centre
Dock Road
Lytham
Lancashire FY8 5AJ
tel: 01253 736334
fax: 01253 795191
sales@sheilamaid.com
(traditional clothes airer, plate
rack and plant stand)

Draks Industries Ltd
Unit 316, Heyford Park
Oxfordshire OX6 3HA
tel: 01869 232989
fax: 01869 232979
(blinds and shutters)

Geoffrey Drayton
85 Hampstead Road
London NW1 2PL
tel: 020 7387 5840
fax: 020 7387 5874
enquiries@geoffrey-
drayton.co.uk
www.geoffrey-drayton.co.uk
(classic modern furniture)

Dyson Appliances
Tetbury Hill
Malmesbury
Wiltshire SN16 0RP
tel: 0870 5275104
fax: 01666 827298
www.dyson.com
(vacuum cleaners)

**Eastern Vision
(Trading) Ltd**
Chequers, The Street
West Clandon
Surrey GU4 7OG
tel: 020 7580 5955
www.EasternVision.com
(hand-made furnishings from
India by mail order)

Fired Earth Ltd
Twyford Mill, Oxford Road
Adderbury
Oxfordshire OX17 3HP
tel: 01295 812088
fax: 01295 810832
uksales@firedearth.com
www.firedearth.com
(tiles, floor coverings,
accessories, paints, bathrooms)

Formica (plastic laminates)
for information ring
0191 259 3000

Habitat UK Ltd (and branches)
196 Tottenham Court Road
London W1P 9LD
tel: 0845 6010740
www.habitat.net

C P Hart
Newnham Terrace
Hercules Road
London SE1 7DR
tel: 020 7902 1000
fax: 020 7902 1001
http://www.cphart.co.uk
(bathrooms and kitchens)

**The Holding Company
Mail Order**
Burlington House
184 New King's Road
London SW6 4NF
tel: 020 7610 9160
fax: 020 7610 9166
mail@theholdingcompany.co.uk
www.theholdingcompany.co.uk
(storage furniture and
accessories)

House
PO Box 1748
Salisbury
Wiltshire SP5 5SP
tel: 01725 552549
fax: 01725 552904
shop@housemailorder.co.uk
www.housemailorder.co.uk
(contemporary accessories)

HSS Hire Service Group
25 Willow Lane
Mitcham
Surrey CR4 4TS
tel: 0845 7282828
fax: 020 8687 5005
hire@hss.co.uk
www.hss.co.uk
(tool and equipment hire:
contact for catalogue and
nearest branch)

Ideal Standard Ltd
The Bathroom Works
National Avenue
Kingston upon Hull
Humberside HU5 4HS
tel: 01482 346461
fax: 01482 445886
www.ideal-standard.co.uk
(bathrooms)

**IKEA Ltd
(and branches)**
255 North Circular Road
London NW10 0JQ
tel: 020 8233 2300

The Inside Edge Catalogue
2 Woburn Street, Ampthill,
Bedfordshire MK45 2HP
tel: 0800 2985793
fax: 01525 840107
theinedge@aol.com
www.the-inside-edge.com
(accessories and gifts)

Jaymart Rubber & Plastics Ltd
Woodland Trading Estate
Eden Vale Road,
Westbury
Wiltshire BA13 3QS
tel: 01373 864926
fax: 01373 858454
jaymart@compuserve.com
(flooring manufacturer
and importer)

Junckers Ltd
Wheaton Court Commercial
Centre, Wheaton Road
Witham, Essex CM8 3UJ
tel: 01376 517512
fax: 01376 514401
www.junckers.co.dk
(hardwood flooring)

Cath Kidston
8 Clarendon Cross
London W11 4AP
tel: 020 7221 4000
fax: 020 7229 1992
(retro textiles and accessories)

Kitschen Sync Mail Order
9 The Pavement
Clapham Common
London SW4 0HY
tel and fax: 020 7720 1609
www.kitschensync.com
(quirky and retro accessories)

Lakeland Ltd
Alexandra Buildings
Windermere,
Cumbria LA23 1BQ
tel: 015394 88100
fax: 015394 88300
www.lakelandlimited.com
(kitchen equipment
and supplies)

London Metal Centre
10 Titan Musiness Estate
Finch Street
London SE8 5QA
tel: 020 8291 7298
fax: 020 8694 2666
artworkmetals@yahoo.com
(sheet metal for flooring,
worksurfaces and splashbacks)

Ian Mankin
109 Regents Park Road
London NW1 8UR
tel: 020 7722 0997
fax: 020 7722 2159
(natural cotton and linen)

Marks & Spencer DIRECT
FREEPOST
PO Box 288
Warrington
Cheshire WA1 2BR
tel: 0845 6031603
fax: 0845 6040604
customer.services@marks-and-
spencer.co.uk
www.marks-and-spencer.co.uk

McCord Design by Mail
London Road
Preston
Lancashire PR11 1RP
tel: 0870 908 7005
fax: 0870 908 7050
www.mccord.uk.com

Herman Miller
149 Tottenham Court Road
London W1P OJA
tel: 020 7388 7331
fax: 020 7387 3507
www.hermanmiller.com
(classic modern furniture)

Monkwell Ltd
10–12 Wharfdale Road
Bournemouth
Dorset BH4 9BT
tel: 01202 752944
fax: 01202 762582
enquiries@monkwell.co
www.monkwell.com
(furnishing fabric manufacturer)

Next Directory
www.next.co.uk
(for shop enquiries
tel: 08702 435435)

Nice Irma's by Post
Unit 2
Finchley Industrial Centre
879 High Road
London N12 8QA
tel: 020 8343 9766
fax: 020 8343 9590
www.niceirmas.com
(exotic textiles and accessories)

Ocean Home Shopping
Freepost
LON811
tel: 0870 2426283
fax: 0870 2426284
www.oceancatalogue.com

OKA Direct Ltd (mail order)
tel: 0870 1606002
fax: 01548 832001
okadirect.com

Paint Magic (Jocasta Innes)
48 Golborne Road
London W10 5PR
tel: 020 8960 9960
fax: 020 8960 9655
www.paint-magic.com
(paints and equipment as
well as courses in decorative
paint effects)

The Pier
for catalogue and customer
orders tel: 020 7814 5004
for store locations
tel: 020 7814 5020

Purves & Purves
81–3 Tottenham Court Road
London W1P 9HD
tel: 0208 453 1827
fax: 020 8961 3443
mailorder@purves.co.uk
www.purves.co.uk
info@purves.co.uk

Roset (UK) Ltd
95 High Street, Great
Missenden
Buckinghamshire HP16 0AL
tel: 01494 865001
fax: 01494 866883
jhigham@ligne-roset.co.uk
(modern furniture
and accessories)

Russell & Chapple
68 Drury Lane
Covent Garden
London WC2B 5SP
tel: 020 7836 7521
fax: 020 7497 0554
(suppliers of artists materials
and a wide selection of low-
cost canvas)

Sanderson
100 Acres
Sanderson Road
Uxbridge
Middlesex UB8 1DH
tel: 01895 201509
fax: 01895 231450
www.sanderson-uk.com
(soft furnishings and
accessories)

Sinclair Till Flooring Co Ltd
791–3 Wandsworth Road
London SW8 3JQ
tel: 020 7720 0031
fax: 020 7498 3814
sinclairtill@lineone.net
(particularly good for linoleum)

Smeg (UK) Ltd
87a Milton Park
Abingdon
Oxfordshire OX14 4RY
tel: 08708 437373
fax: 08708 464040
www.smeguk.com
(domestic appliances)

Solid Floor
128 John Street
London EC1V 4JS
tel: 020 7251 2917
fax: 020 7253 7419
solidfloor@dircom.co.uk
www.solidfloor.uk
(timber and bamboo flooring)

Space Boudoir
214 Westbourne Grove
London W11 2RH
tel: 020 7229 6533
fax: 020 7727 0134
boudoir@spaceshop.co.uk
www.spaceshop.co.uk
(bedroom accessories and
hand-embroidered bedlinen)

Space2
FREEPOST CL3341
PO Box 99, Sudbury
Suffolk CO10 6BR
tel: 0800 0282022
fax: 01787 378426
info@space2.com
www.space2.com
(home-office furniture)

VI-SPRING Ltd
Ernesettle Lane
Ernesettle
Plymouth PL5 2TT
tel: 01752 366311
fax: 01752 355108
info@vispring.co.uk
(hand-made bed manufacturer)

Volga Linen Company
Unit 1D
Eastland Road Industrial Estate
Leiston
Suffolk IP16 4LL
tel: 01728 635020
fax: 01728 635021
volgalinen@aol.com
www.volgelinen.co.uk
(pure linen bed, table and
kitchen linen)

The White Company
Unit 30, Perivale Industrial Park
Horsenden Lane South
Greenford, Middlesex UB6 7RJ
tel: 08701 601610
fax: 0870 160 1611
orders@thewhitecompany.co.uk
(white bath, bed and table
linen, china and accessories)

Christopher Wray Lighting
591–3 King's Road
London SW6 2YW
tel: 020 7736 8434
fax: 020 7731 3507
sales@christopher-wray.com
www.christopher-wray.com
(comprehesive range of lighting
and accessories such as bulbs
and flex)

Websites

www.bluedeco.com
(wide range of stylish
household products)

www.chiasmus.co.uk
(quirky accessories)

www.hirevolution.co.uk
(directory of services, from
architects to plumbers and
decorators)

www.interiorinternet.com
(designer furnishings, some
exclusive)

www.letsbuyit.com
(general discount site
with impressive House and
Garden section)

Useful Addresses

Federation of Master Builders
14–15 Great James Street
London WC1N 3DP
tel: 020 7242 7583
fax: 020 7404 0296
www.fmb.org.uk

**National Federation of
Painting and Decorating**
Contractors
82 New Cavendish Street
London W1M 9FG
(apply in writing)

**Royal Institute of British
Architects**
66 Portland Place
London W1N 4AD
tel: 020 7580 5533
fax: 020 7631 1802
bal@inst.riba.org
www.architecture.com

index

Figures in italics indicate captions.

picture credits

The publishers would like to thank the following sources for their kind permission to reproduce the pictures in this book:

Astracast plc 144t, 145
Bisque Radiators 14/15
Bombay Duck 103, 104t, 108
Carlton Books Ltd/Graham Atkins-Hughes 47/Janine Hosegood 45, 93
Corbis/Historical Picture Archive 28b, 28t/Kevin R Morris 33
Crosslee plc 150b
Crown Paints 63tl, 63btl
Crucial Trading/courtesy of Lara Grylls PR 72, 74
Cucina Direct/courtesy of Caroline Bourke Communications 152, 153, 154, 155, 171, 173
The Decorative Fabrics Gallery/courtesy of Monkwell Press Office 99
DIY Photo Library 63mtl
The Domestic Paraphernalia Company 150t
Dyson 157b
Fired Earth 59, 61, 72/3, 80, 204r, 206tr
Getty One Stone 169b, 170
Habitat UK Ltd 48, 54, 159, 163, 168/169, 169tr
The Holding Company/courtesy of Camron Public Relations 165, 191, 192, 193b, 209br, 209tr
Ideal-Standard Ltd 198
Ikea/courtesy of Condor Public Relations 137, 146
Image Bank 46
Jocasta Innes/Paint Magic Ltd 63br
The Interior Archive/Fritz von der Schulenburg/Designer: Jasper Conran 202

Interlubke courtesy of Geoffrey Drayton 177b
IPC Syndication 40/1, 63tc, 63bl
IPC Syndication/Caroline Arber/Homes & Gardens 49
IPC Syndication/Tom Leighton/Living etc 9, 132, 187
IPC Syndication/David Montgomery/Homes & Gardens 185
IPC Syndication/Lucy Pope/Homes & Gardens 104b
IPC Syndication/Nick Pope/Living etc 189
IPC Syndication/Trevor Richards/Homes & Gardens 183
IPC Syndication/Pia Tryde/Homes & Gardens 44r, 174
IPC Syndication/Chris Tubbs/Living etc 193t, 195
IPC Syndication/Mark Williams/Homes & Gardens
IPC Syndication/Polly Wreford/Homes & Gardens 11, 98, 102t, 102b, 166, 205br, 205tl, 207r, 207l
Ligne Roset (UK) Ltd 119t, 119b, 121t, 123, 161, 162
Ray Main/Mainstream 6, 10, 18, 20, 21, 22/23, 29, 32, 35, 39, 50/51, 55, 57, 58, 66, 75, 78/79, 86, 88, 90, 91, 92, 96/97, 101t, 107, 109, 112, 113, 116b, 117, 124b, 127, 128, 134, 135, 136, 139, 140l, 142, 147tl, 149, 177t, 182, 196, 199, 200, 201t, 203, 204l, 205bl, 206tl, 209tl, 216
Ray Main/Mainstream/Designer: Nick Allen 76
Ray Main/Mainstream/Designer: Babylon Design 129, 141
Ray Main/Mainstream/Architects: Sergison Bates 131
Ray Main/Mainstream/Designer: Ozwald Boateng 30, 34
Ray Main/Mainstream/Designer: Bobo 94/95
Ray Main/Mainstream/Designer: Henrietta Burnett 106
Ray Main/Mainstream/Architects: Circus 147tr, 214

Ray Main/Mainstream/ Designer: Jasper Conran 96
Ray Main/Mainstream/Designer: Orianna Fielding-Banks 143
Ray Main/Mainstream/Designer: Andrew Folkes 140r, 144b, 156
Ray Main/Mainstream/Architect: Spencer Fung 16, 178
Ray Main/Mainstream/Designer: Kelly Hoppen 67
Ray Main/Mainstream/Architect: Sabiha Malik 138
Ray Main/Mainstream/Architect: Andrew Martin FAT Architects 116t
Ray Main/Mainstream/Designer: Martin Lee Associates 71
Ray Main/Mainstream/Designer: Mathmos 6, 122, 125t, 130t, 210, 211
Ray Main/Mainstream/Designer: Katherine Memmi 158
Ray Main/Mainstream/Designer: John Minshaw Designs 208, 217
Ray Main/Mainstream/Designer: Clare Nash 126cl
Ray Main/Mainstream/Designer: Roger Oates 17, 118
Ray Main/Mainstream/Architect: John Pawson 212
Ray Main/Mainstream/Architect: Nico Rensch 24/5
Ray Main/Mainstream/Architect: Charles Rutherfoord 176
Ray Main/Mainstream/Designer: Michael Sodeaux 83
Ray Main/Mainstream/Designer: Helen Tindale 12
Ray Main/Mainstream/Designer: Vincent Wolfe 101b
Ocean 105, 111, 121b, 123br, 130b
Paul Ryan/ International Interiors/ Designer: Jan Des Bouvrie 127b
Paul Ryan/International Interiors/ Designer: Nick Dine 190
Paul Ryan/International Interiors/ Moneo & Brock Architects 213
Paul Ryan/International Interiors/

Designer: Jacqueline Morabito 81
Paul Ryan/International Interiors/ Designer: Kristina & Bjorn Sahlquist 215
Paul Ryan/International Interiors/ Designer: Alexander Vethers 27
Paul Ryan/International Interiors/ Designer: Sasha Waddell 52
The Pier/courtesy of Camron Public Relations 120t, 120b, 124t, 172, 194
Purves & Purves 157t, 164
Sanderson 2, 38, 42, 43, 44c, 44l, 57bl, 64, 65, 84, 175, 184, 188
Smeg (UK) Ltd/courtesy of Publicity Engineers 148, 151
Solid Floor 77
Verne/Els Lybeer & Thomas Siffer (owners), Wim De Puydt (architect) 26
VI-SPRING Ltd/courtesy of Sheppard Day 179, 180l, 181, 186
The White Company, London 197
Wools of New Zealand/Parker Hobart Associates 110, 114

A special thank you is due to Owen at Mainstream and to everyone who kindly supplied images for the book.

Every effort has been made to acknowledge correctly and contact the source and/or copyright holder of each picture, and Carlton Books Limited apologizes for any unintentional errors or omissions, which will be corrected in future editions of this book.

author's acknowledgements

My sincere appreciation to everyone at Carlton Books for their enthusiasm, flair and very hard work. In particular I would like to thank Venetia Penfold for commissioning Setting Up Home; Zia Mattocks for supervising its progress with a skilled eye and an unfailingly sweet nature; Jane Donovan for processing and advising on a huge number of words with enormous grace and speed; Barbara Zuñiga, with Joanne Long, for making sense of a hugely diverse collection of facts and ideas with their striking and stylish design; and Alex Pepper for unearthing a unique and inspiring collection of photographic images.

For their constant and reliable support, I am also extremely grateful to Robert Breckman, Lloyd Reynolds and my agent Barbara Levy, whose calm demeanour and wise counsel I depend on.